CW00864432

The Obituary Book

Published at www.lulu.com
May 2013

'I give to each child the right to choose a star that shall be his ... and all meadows, with the clover blooms and butterflies thereof, and all woods'

From the famous last wishes of 'Charles Lounsbury', whose literary creator was Williston J Fish (1858-1939). The words of Williston J Fish live on, but little can be discovered of the man who gave each child a star

INTRODUCTION

TWO websites, The ROCK (www.irelandrock.com) and The Obituary Book (www.theobituarybook.com) were published online in 2010 and 2013 respectively. The former is now obsolete; the latter will soon follow suit. The concept of both sites was to create a central source of obituaries for easy reference and preservation; in simplistic terms, a static 'Facebook':

Leave Something Behind

Rarely can we discover much of someone's life beyond the span of birth and death, and sometimes, even that information eludes us. Life is an accumulation of stories told, retold, and all too often, untold. The Obituary Book aims to preserve those recollections for the families and genealogists of the future.

The Obituary Book was not restricted by date or time, retrospective obituaries were invited from authors in all parts of the globe. It invited users to compose their own obituaries if desired. Both projects failed, neither site elicited one response. However, a significant quantity of material was created by the authors to illustrate the site concept and is recorded here for its historical interest.

**Janet Murphy, Killarney &
Eileen Chamberlain, UK
May 2013**

AHN, Dr Imsoo (unknown date to 2010)

KERRY is not the place you would expect to find an obituary to a lady from South Korea, whose only link to the county is her friendship with this author. But here she must be placed, for too little of her life in Korea is known to place it there. Dr Ahn, aka Chung-a, professor of English literature, is to be commended for delivering Irish literature to an Eastern audience. We met in 2005, the year WB Yeats was knocked down by a car, a hit and run as far as I can recall (the incident occurred during the Yeats Summer School in Co Sligo, which we were both attending. It caused some excitement to witness Yeats (the statued version) reduced to pieces during his 'own' festival.) I noticed Imsoo immediately; she was the sort of person who filled a room: sun-like energy, her dress a flower garden of colour. We got talking during an organized excursion to Queen Maeve's tomb on Knocknarea when I noticed she trailed behind. Imsoo confided that despite her energy, she was sick, her chest scarred like a spaghetti junction from heart surgery (her words). We abandoned the walk and sat instead in the car park chatting like sisters (she afterwards always addressed me as sister because she believed we had always known each other). We swapped stories; she told me of life in Korea, her marriage to her career, how she was often escorted out of her workplace at Kwandong University by the caretaker in the early hours, always last to leave. Those few short days in Sligo forged our friendship. In the years that followed we emailed, wrote and spoke on the telephone. She was passionate about Lady Gregory and in 2006, with permission from Sam McCready, worked on a translation of Coole Lady. The book was published in Korean in summer 2007. During this time her health prevented her from returning to Ireland but in 2008, she once again made the trip to Sligo to continue her research of Lady Gregory, full of plans for more translations. She also spent a week with me in Kerry. She arrived by coach, loaded with books, full of zest, and raring to see all there was of the county. We visited the lakes, waterfalls, took a jaunting trip through the Gap, and trawled every bookshop. But behind her outward energy, her frailty was more evident and on her return to South Korea, she was taken from the plane by ambulance to hospital where she remained for many weeks. She returned to work, and in 2009 was requesting essays from colleagues for a planned book to mark her retirement. I was to attend the grand event. I last spoke to her in the early part of this year (2010), her voice then was barely audible. She was very ill, staying with her brother and his wife, but as ever hoped soon to return to work. She had so much unfinished business. In July, one of my letters was returned unopened. I telephoned; the line was out of service. I emailed; it bounced back. I contacted her university, and learned she had died of sickness 'some months ago'. Without names, addresses, language, I am unable to condole with Dr Ahn's family, friends, colleagues. I can only hope that her beloved Coole Lady is taking good care of her.

Composed by Janet Murphy, Killarney, on 14 September 2010 (R3)

BOUCICAULT, Dion (1820-1890)

MR DION Boucicault died in New York on Thursday of pneumonia, after a lingering illness, in the seventieth year of his age. The news came yesterday as a surprise to many who only lately heard of Mr Boucicault as a newspaper controversialist and as the author of a recently produced play. The extraordinary fecundity of the deceased dramatist, and the ease with which he adapted himself to various styles of dramatic composition, were little less than marvellous. Though Boucicault was a practised playwright in the exact sense of the word, there is more than mere mechanical carpentering in most of his works; and the more popular of them have stood the test of time wonderfully well. With unflagging spirits, a never-failing supply of humour, and enough literary power to satisfy the intelligent playgoer, Boucicault was able to please the public without descending to the level of the mere hack dramatist. He was born at Dublin on Dec 26th 1820; and in 1841 his comedy of London Assurance was played at Covent-garden Theatre by a company including Madame Vestris, Mrs Nesbitt, William Farren, James Anderson and Charles Mathews. The piece was immediately successful and the year after Boucicault, abandoning the nom de theatre of 'Lee Morton' under which London Assurance was produced, brought out, at the same theatre, and under his own name, The Irish Heiress, which was not very well received. Alma Mater; or a Cure for Coquettes, performed at the Haymarket in September 1842 had a more favourable reception, but his next effort, Woman, produced at Covent-garden, was less satisfactory. Old Heads and Young Hearts, at the Haymarket in 1844, displayed much of the wit and ingenuity that had made London Assurance acceptable. A School for Scheming at the Haymarket in 1847, Confidence at the same theatre in 1848, The Knight of Arva also at the Haymarket in the latter year, The Broken Vow at the Olympic in 1851 and The Queen of Spades at Drury-lane in the same year were none of them very successful, three of them being adaptations. In June 1852 Mr Boucicault made his debut as an actor at the Princess's Theatre in a piece of his own called The Vampire. In this he played the title-part. In the same year he produced at the Princess's his play of The Prima Donna, which was followed in 1853 at the Adelphi by his adaptation called Genevieve, shortly after he went to New York where he brought out, also in 1853, his drama called The Fox Hunt and in 1854, his version of Delavigne's Louis XI. To this succeeded, in 1855 his Eugenic at Drury-lane and his Janet Pride at the

Adelphi, with Madame Celeste in the title-part. After this came George Darville at the Adelphi in 1857 and then The Colleen Bawn at the same theatre in 1860, with the author as Myles-na-Coppaleen (sic), his wife (Agnes Robertson) as Eily O'Connor, and Mr and Mrs Billington, Mrs Alfred Mellon, Edmund Falconer and David Fisher in other parts. This production at once settled Boucicault's rank both as an author and an actor, and was the foundation of his popularity and fame. The Colleen Bawn, founded on Griffin's novel of 'The Collegians', was an admirable specimen of stage craft. In 1861 came The Octoroon at the Adelphi with Boucicault as Salem Scudder, another great popular success. The Dublin Boy, The Life of an Actress, Dot, and The Relief of Lucknow all came out in London in 1862, Dot being a version of The Cricket on the Hearth. In 1863 The Trial of Effie Deans and The Streets of London were performed; in 1865, Arrah-na-pogue, with himself as Shaun; in 1866 The Parish Clerk, The Long Strike, The Flying Scud and Hunted Down. After Dark appeared in 1868, and presumptive Evidence in 1869, in which latter year, Formosa was first seen at Drury-lane. It was followed by Paul Lafarge, A Dark Night's Work, The Rapparee, and Jezebel – all in 1870; Night and Morning in 1872, Led Astray in 1874 and The Shaughraun in 1875. In 1879 Rescued was produced at the Adelphi and in 1880, The Bridal Tour at the Haymarket; Forbidden Fruit and The O'Dowd (the two latter both at the Adelphi). In 1881 came Mimi, at the Court, and in 1886 at the Prince's, The Jilt, in which Mr Boucicault made his last appearance in England as an actor. Recent productions of Boucicault's were Fin Mac Coull, Phrync, The Tale of a Coat, only recently noticed in our columns. Boucicault was educated at Dublin University under the care of his guardian, Dr Lardner,

and at the London University. Two of his sons, Messrs
Dion G and Aubrey Boucicault, are on the stage.

The Era, 20 September 1890 (R33). Boucicault's play The
Colleen Bawn, based on Griffin's Collegians, dramatised the
alleged murder of Ellen Hanley by John Scanlan and Stephen
Sullivan. Both men were executed in 1820. See note at entry
Michael John WHITTY for an earlier version of events which
has been reproduced with footnotes.

BOXOLD, Frederick Edwin J

AFTER REQUIEM High Mass for the repose of his soul,
at the Cathedral, Killarney on Monday, the remains of
the late Sergt Boxall (sic) killed in the ambush near
Millstreet, were interred in the new cemetery, Killarney
with full military honours. A large number of civilians
attended the funeral and while the cortege passed
through the town all business windows were closed.
Father Fitzgerald assisted by Father O'Sullivan assisted
at the graveside.

The Kerryman, 19 February 1921 (R74)

BROWNE, Valentine Augustus (1825-1905) 4th Earl of
Kenmare, son of Sir Thomas Browne and Catherine
O'Callaghan, husband of Gertrude Harriet Thynne and
father of Valentine Charles

THE DEATH of the Right Hon the Earl of Kenmare,
KP, took place at his London residence at eight o'clock
on Thursday evening. The deceased Earl, who was
within a few months of his 80th anniversary, had been
seriously ill for a few days, and became unconscious on
Thursday morning. The noble Earl was born on 16th
May 1825 and sat in Parliament as Liberal member for
County Kerry from 1852 to 1871, when he succeeded to
the title on the death of the third Earl of Kenmare. He
was Comptroller of the Household, 1851-58; Vice
Chamberlain 1859-66, 1868-72; Lord-in-Waiting 1872-
74, and Lord Chamberlain 1880-86. In 1858 he was
married to Gertrude, only daughter of Lord Charles
Thynne. He owned no less than 13,000 acres in
Ireland, and is succeeded by his son, Viscount

Castlerosse. The now deceased Earl was the fourth
Eaqrl of Kenmare and was Lord Lieutenant of the
County Kerry since 1866. He became Hon Colonel of
the 4th battalion Royal Munster Fusiliers (The Kerry
Militia) in 1866. he was also a Senator of the Royal
University of Ireland. For many years he pla7ed a
prominent part in public affairs in this his native county
and in the public life of the country generally. He was
associated with various public boards where his efforts
were directed towards progress and economic
administration. He was a Roman Catholic, and always
contributed generously to the charities and institutions of
his Church. The late Earl entertained Queen Victoria
and the Prince Consort on the occasion of their visit to
the lakes in August 1861 and he afterwards had as
guests the present King and Queen when Prince and
Princess of Wales, and subsequently the Duke and
Duchess of York, now Prince and Princess of Wales.
Those interested in the Munster Feis will hear with
feelings of the deepest regret of the death of the Earl of
Kenmare. Last year he welcomed this Festival to
Killarney by giving permission to the Committee to hold
it in his beautiful demesne and by giving it generous
support in other ways. Indeed the late Earl was one of
the most interested of the visitors to the Feis grounds
last August and especially was he pleased at the
brightness and spirit displayed by those who sought to
secure handsome and valuable medals offered in th
dancing competitions. Killarney Gaelic Leaguers will
mourn his loss, and on behalf of the Munster Feis
Committee the Chairman and Secretary wish to join in
the universal regret caused by the death of one who has
not only proved a kind and generous patron, but also a
thorough supporter of the revival of our language and
pastimes. The remains of the late Earl arrived at

Killarney by the 12 o'clock train on Monday, and were met at the railway station by an extremely large concourse of people representative of all creeds and classes who accompanied them to Killarney House. The order of processions was as follows: the children of Presentation Convent dressed in black with white veils tied with crepe came first, then the children of the Mercy Convent followed by the Industrial School children, then the children of the Presentation Monastery Schools, all wearing mourning badges. The Most Rev Dr Mangan in his carriage, and the clergy preceded the remains which were placed on a bier and drawn by boatmen wearing his lordship's uniform. Immediately after the remains walked Lord Castlerosse and Mr Greville Douglas. Then came the general public, and a contingent of the Royal Irish Constabulary. As the procession passed through the town via the Franciscan Monastery, College Street, Henn Street, Main Street, New Street and Presentation Convent, there were signs of mourning on all sides. All the shops were closely shuttered, business was suspended, and blinds were drawn in private houses as a mark of respect to the deceased Earl. Shortly after 10 o'clock on Wednesday morning the body of the late Earl was removed from Killarney House. The funeral was an immense one and very representative of the whole county. His Majesty the King was represented by Major General Pole-Carew and the Lord Lieutenant of Ireland had also a representative present. The long procession proceeded from Killarney House through the Demesne reaching the town by way of Kenmare Place the thence through Main Street and New Street to the Cathedral. All places of business were closed. At the Cathedral Office for the dead and Requiem High Mass was gone through and the coffin was afterwards interred in the family vault in the Cathedral.

Obituary from *The Kerry Evening Post* 11 & 15 February 1905 **(R19)**

Earl of Kenmare: The Will of the late Earl of Kenmare

'The Right Hon Valentine Augustus, fourth Earl of Kenmare, KP, PC, and Baron Kenmare in the peerage of the United Kingdom, of Killarney House, Killarney, Ireland, Liberal MP for Kerry 1852-71, Controller of the Household and Lord Chamberlain to her late Majesty, High Sheriff for Kerry 1851, and Lord Lieutenant of the county since 1866, and who died at the Hans Crescent Hotel, London SW, on the 9th February last, aged 79 years, left estate of the gross value of £132,258 18s 10dm with net personality nil. Probate of his will of the 22nd July 1901 has been granted to his son, the Right Hon Valentine Charles, fifth Earl of Kenmare, of Killarney House, Killarney. The testator bequeathed to his wife, Gertrude Harriet (daughter of Lord Charles Thynne), in addition to provision made for her by settlements, £1,000, and to his sister, Lady Ellen Maria Browne, £200, and to his daughter, Lady Margaret Douglas, £200, for the purchase of momentoes [*sic*], and regretted that he could make no further provision for them, as 'my estate in Ireland has considerably diminished.' To Miss Connery, formerly in his service, he bequeathed £100, and left all the rest and residue of his estate to his said son, the present Earl of Kenmare, absolutely.'

The Kerry Evening Star, 30 March 1905

BROWNE, Valentine Charles, 5th Earl of Kenmare (1860-1941) son of Valentine Augustus Browne and Gertrude Harriet Thynne, husband of Elizabeth Baring, and father of Valentine Edward, 6th Earl

CHARLES Valentine (sic), 6th Earl of Kenmare was laid to rest in the family vault under Our Lady's Chapel in St Mary's Cathedral after Pontifical Requiem High Mass, celebrated by Most Rev Dr M O'Brien, Bishop of Kerry. All business in the town was suspended and schools and convents closed. The Cathedral had an overflow congregation, including representatives of all the public bodies in the County Kerry and different organisations. The new Earl, Viscount Castlerosse, was seated on the ancestral chair in the High Altar, while Major the Hon Gerald Browne, third son, was also accommodated in a special seat in the High Altar, where on a catafalque, the coffin rested, covered with wreaths. Owing to the precarious state of her health, the Countess of Kenmare was forbidden to attend by her doctors. After the Mass workmen of the Estate shouldered the coffin to Our Lady's Altar, which was draped in black, and lowered it into the family vault, where it was placed between the late Earl's father and mother. The first Earl was interred there in 1812. When the remains arrived from Dublin this morning they were received by His Lordship, the Bishop of Kerry, Very Rev J Slattery, Adm, VP and Rev P O'Sullivan, CC.

Extract from *The Kerryman*, November 1941 (R20)

BROWNE, Valentine Edward, 6th Earl of Kenmare
(1891-1943) son of Valentine Charles Browne and
Elizabeth Baring, husband of Doris Delavigne (1st wife)
and Enid Lindeman

VALENTINE Edward Charles Browne, sixth Earl of
Kenmare, is dead. He had a heart attack on Sunday
evening, and on Monday he passed away. Lord
Kenmare was better known to Ireland and the world as

Viscount Castlerosse, whose literary genius made him universally famous. On the death of his father he succeeded to the title in November 1941. Last January he married Lady Furness, and in June they took up residence at the ancestral home in Killarney. Last week Lady Kenmare returned to London on holiday. The news of the rather sudden and unexpected demise of such a true and staunch friend left everyone in Killarney stunned. Genial, kind, lovable, and charitable, he was held in the highest esteem by all and his passing away has left a void which will always remain. Full of intellectual vigour, aided by a dynamic driving force, his unsparing efforts towards the advancement of Killarney have produced results which are immeasurable. Killarney seemed to be his chief concern in life. He was always planning and planning for a brighter and better tourist centre, and he left no stone unturned in his efforts to make a Paradise of 'Beauty's Home'. Perhaps his greatest work and that which will remain as an imposing memorial to him was the laying of the beautiful lakeside 18-hole Golf Links, reputed to be the finest in Europe. He made a splendid job of this but was never satisfied that it had reached perfection. He was always on the look-out for improvements and every day saw it becoming still more magnificent. He sought the advice of the best golf course experts in Europe and quite recently almost succeeded in getting famous Henry Cotton over. A few months ago he had as guest the Curator of Kew Gardens, London and with him devised a scheme for the planting of millions of flowers and shrubs on various parts of the links to produce a massive display of colour. The project was actually launched a few days ago when a consignment of 6,000 plants arrived. It is a tragedy indeed that he should pass away when his plans were about to blossom forth

and it is without doubt the hardest blow which Killarney
has received for a long, long time. Every organisation
and movement for the advancement of the town had his
unflinching support. He also had in mind the idea of
creating an airport at Killarney. Most of this summer he
had spent deerstalking at Killarney. He had also
frequent business conferences about the development
of his 10,000 acre Killarney estate. The Race Company
also received invaluable assistance from him and a
good measure of the success of Killarney Races is due
to him. It is probably understatement to say that he did
as much for the development of Killarney as anyone
ever did in the history of the town. Yet it was only an
intimate few that were aware of his labour of love. He
moved silently yet forcefully and steadily behind the
scenes, and unrelentingly he pursued to the last his
life's task in adorning and developing what was to him
the most beautiful spot on earth. Returning to London
after the last war, in which as captain in the Irish Guards
he was severely wounded, he entered the banking
business for a period but soon turned to Fleet Street
where as a journalist he won a great following. He was
best known for his widely-read 'Londoner's Log'. He
was a director of the Evening Standard, the Daily
Express and the Sunday Express. The remains of the
late Earl of Kenmare today lie in the peaceful seclusion
of the family burial vault in St Mary's Cathedral, but his
living link with Killarney will always remain an abiding
and undying memory with those who knew the
greatness of this great man and his unswerving and
loyal devotion to his home town. A great mind has
ceased its work, a great builder has laid his tools aside
for the last time with his life's labour of love cut short on
the eve of its fulfilment. The death of Lord Castlerosse,
as he will always be remembered, is more than a

national loss; it is a national tragedy, an event that will be mourned for many, many years by those who knew what his master mind and magnetic charm meant to Irish tourism. For Killarney, his passing is a disaster; a catastrophe which cannot be measured. The town went into deep mourning for his funeral. All business houses were closed and blinds were drawn in all windows as the cortege passed through the streets en route to the Cathedral. Thousands of people followed the bier, which was drawn by employees of the Kenmare estate. A representative congregation numbering over one thousand attended a Solemn Mass of Requiem for the late Lord Kenmare at Westminster Cathedral. Previous to the ceremony a selection of plaintive Irish airs, including 'Oft in the Stilly Night', was rendered by the Cathedral organist. The widow of the deceased, Lady Kenmare, was present but the Dowager Countess was unable to attend owing to illness.

Extracted from *The Kerryman*, 25th September 1943 & 2nd October 1943 (R21)

BROWNE, Gerald Ralph Desmond, 7th Earl of Kenmare (1896-1952) Third son of Valentine Charles Browne and Elizabeth Baring

GERALD Ralph Desmond Browne, OBE, 7th Earl of Kenmare died this morning at his Killarney residence, Killarney House. Unmarried and the last surviving son of the 5th Earl, the title dies with him. He was born on December 20 1896 and was educated at the Oratory School. He served in the Great War from 1916 to 1919 and retired from the army with the rank of Major. He was ADC to the Lieut-General and Gov-General of Ireland in 1921. He succeeded to the title in 1943 on the death of his brother, the 6th Earl, better known as Lord Castlerosse, the journalist. He is survived by two sisters Lady Dorothy Margaret Charteris to whom the Killarney estate passes and Lady Cecilia Kathleen Vesey who is a lady-in-waiting to Queen Mary. Prior to his prolonged illness the Earl took a keen interest in Killarney affairs and was at the time of his death

President of Killarney Tourist Association, President of Killarney Golf Club, President of the Co Kerry Ploughing Association, President of Killarney Show Society and Patron of the Killarney Ploughing Society. The remains will be removed to St Mary's Cathedral, Killarney on Sunday at 4pm from Killarney House. Solemn Requiem Mass on Monday at 11am. The funeral will take place immediately afterwards to the family vault in the Blessed Virgin's Chapel in the Cathedral.

Extract from *The Kerryman*, February 16 1952 (R22)

BUSTEED, John Esq

DIED, MRS Busteed, widow of late John Busteed Esq, founder of the Kerry Evening Post, age 76, mother of Late Morgan O C Busteed, MD.

Kerry Evening Post, 3 March 1830

Note: Notice of death of John Busteed of Tralee Esq proprietor of Kerry Evening Post published in Gentleman's Magazine of January to June 1819 under the death notices for March 1819. John and Catherine Busteed would appear to have been the parents of: Richard (baptised 1783), William (baptised 1784), John (baptised 1788), Morgan O'Connell (baptised 1790), Frances (baptised 1793), Barbara (baptised 1794), Thomas Ellis Emmett (baptised 1797). In his will made 23 January 1830, Morgan O'Connell Busteed Esq, Surgeon of the Kerry Regiment of Militia at Tralee, made bequests to his wife Ellen, brother John, sisters Barbara and Bridget and brothers-in-law John James Hickson Esq (or Dickson) and Robert David Fitzgerald Esq and the Kerry Bible Society which included property at Strand Street and a field named

Arbutus. His will was witnessed by Wm Fitzgerald, Thomas Spring, Thomas Payne. Administration was granted to his widow Ellen on 31st August 1830. Morgan O'Connell Busteed Esq was patron of Ballinvoher school in Kerry and John Busteed Esq patron of Ballygarron school in Kerry (see Twelfth Report of Society for Promoting the Education of the Poor of Ireland, 1824). 'Died, Barbara Knox, wife of John B Knox Esq and odo late John Busteed Esq' (*Kerry Evening Post*, 25 January 1837).

Following document held at the National Archives of Ireland (Chief Secretary's Office Registered Papers) suggests that a son of John Busteed Esq may have continued the newspaper: 'Letter from John Busteed, 'Kerry Evening Post' office, Tralee, County Kerry, proprietor of 'Kerry Evening Post', to Charles Grant, Chief Secretary, Dublin Castle, concerning reports he has heard of government's intention to withdraw its patronage from the 'Kerry Evening Post' newspaper following his stance in a recent local controversy. Describes and defends his defence of Methodists from the antipathy of the local Anglican curate, concerning the Methodist school in Tralee, 28 September 1819. Encloses newspaper cutting from 'Kerry Evening Post', of article Busteed published in defence of the Methodists and denouncing the actions of the curate involved, [September 1819].'

COLOMB, Sir John Charles Ready (1838-1909)

THE RIGHT Hon Sir John Colomb died at seven o'clock on Thursday night at his London residence, 75 Belgrave Square, SW. He had been ill for the past three weeks and had undergone a serious operation. Sir John Charles Ready Colomb, who was born in May 1838, was a son of General George Thomas Colomb. He was educated privately, and entered the Royal Naval College from which he passed in 1854 into the Royal Marine Artillery, retiring with the rank of Captain in 1869. During his period of service he was variously employed with the Navy, Army, Militia, and Volunteers. This early career supplied the incentive of nearly all his work both before the after he entered public life. Before he was returned in the Conservative interest to Parliament for the Bow and Bromley Division of the Tower Hamlets, in

1882, a seat which he retained till 1892, he had begun to issue the remarkable series of books and pamphlets by which he exercised a strong influence on public opinion. He travelled much abroad, and as early as 1873 he had drawn attention to the question of Colonial defence. He was one of the founders of the Imperial Federation League, and on the platform and by his pen he powerfully pleaded the cause to which this organisation was devoted. In the House of Commons he was always attentively listened to, and his broad sides on Naval affairs gained him the title of 'Reverberating Colomb'. After his defeat in Bow and Bromley in 1892, he was one of the House for three years. In 1895, after a stiff fight, he defeated an Admiral's son at Great Yarmouth and in 1900 the borough returned him without a contest. He did not seek re-election in 1906. As an Irish landowner of 4,500 acres at Dromquinna, Kenmare, Co Kerry, Sir John took a keen interest in Irish affairs, and he rendered valuable services to this country, not only in Parliament, but on various Commissions of Inquiry. He was Chairman of the Appeals Commission under the Local Government (Ireland) Act 1898, a member of Royal Commission on the Supply of Food in Time of War, and a member of Lord Dudley's Congested Districts Commission, which issued its report last year. During the protracted labours of the Congested Inquiry he very rarely missed a sitting, and always displayed a keen interest in the work of investigation. While looking closely after the landlord interests, he never overlooked the claims of the tenants, his views being always tolerant and based on an anxious desire to solve satisfactorily the question of congestion. It is interesting to recall the fact that Lord

Dudley and he were responsible for an agreeable departure from the usual procedure adopted at the sittings, and they permitted smoking during the hearing of evidence. When the findings of the Commission were published last year Sir John Colomb, in addition to signing the majority report, issued a special memorandum, which attracted much attention. Although in general agreement with the Commission, he felt bound to express opinion with regard to the economic effect of breaking up and redistributing the grass lands, the constitution of the Courts regarding compulsory acquisition and the nature of the primary education best calculated to fit the children of the agricultural class. He stated that he could not support the proposal to break up the grass lands unless it was strictly limited to the area which was recognised as congested. He dissented from the arguments favouring the abolition of the grazing system founded upon theories, and failing to recognise sufficiently the economic value of these great grazing tracts to the small holders. As regards the constitution of the Courts to settle matters arising out of compulsory acquisition, Sir John Colomb held that it would not tend to the security of property and he also emphasised the necessity of agricultural education as in his opinion it was an essential condition for the real relief of congestion that the minds and energies of the people should be directed to making the best use of the land they occupied. Sir John Colomb published 'Protection of Commerce in War' in 1867, 'Imperial Strategy' in the following year, 'The Distributions of Our War Forces' in 1869, 'Colonial Defence and Colonial Opinions' in 1873, 'The Defence of Great and Greater Britain' 1879, 'Naval Intelligence and Protection of Commerce' 1881, 'The Use and Application of Marine Forces' 1883, 'Imperial Federation, Naval and Military' 1886, 'British Defence 1800-1900', 'British Dangers' 'Our Ships, Colonies and Commerce in War' were among the most recent of his publications. Sir John Colomb, who was very popular with all classes in Kerry, was a Deputy Lieutenant and a Justice of Peace for the county; and in 1895 served the office of High Sheriff. In the year 1886 he received the KCMG and six years later he was nominated to the Privy Council in Ireland. In 1866 he married Emily Anna, daughter of R S Palmer, and widow of Charles Augustus Paget, Lieutenant of the Royal Navy. He leaves one son, Rupert P, and two daughters, Mrs Smyth and Mrs Snaggs. A service to the memory of Sir John Colomb was held in St Margaret's Church, Westminster. The service was conducted by the Rev C Knox and many old colleagues and comrades of Sir John were present. This was particularly so with regard to the navy. Most members of Parliament are out of town at the moment or more of Sir John's colleagues in the last Parliament would have been present. Amongst those in the church were Vice-Admiral Sir J Durnford, Major-General Adair, Lord Kenmare, Sir R U Penrose-Fitzgerald, Lord MacDonnell, and Admiral Sir Reginald Custance.

Obituary published in *The Kerry Evening Post*, 29th May & 2nd & 5th June 1909 (R15)

CURRAN, John Philpot (1750-1817)

ON TUESDAY evening, at nine o'clock, at his apartments at Brompton, died the Right Honourable John Philpot Curran. He is almost the last of that brilliant phalanx, the contemporaries, and fellow-labourers of Mr Fox, in the cause of general liberty. Lord Erskine, in this country, and Mrs Grattan, in Ireland, still survive. Mr Curran is one of those characters which the lover of human nature, and of its intellectual capacities, delights to contemplate. He rose from nothing. He derived no aid from rank and fortune. He ascended by his own energies to an eminence, which throws rank and fortune into comparative scorn. Mr Curran was the great ornament of his time of the Irish bar, and in forensic eloquence has certainly never been exceeded in modern times. His rhetoric was the pure emanation of his spirit, a warming and lighting up of the soul that poured conviction and astonishment on his hearers. It flashed in his eye, and revelled in the melodious and powerful accents of his voice. His thoughts almost always shaped themselves into imagery, and if his eloquence had any fault, it was that his images were too frequent. But they were at the same time so exquisitely beautiful, that he must have been a rigorous critic, that could have determined which of them to part with. His wit was not less exuberant than his imagination; and it was the peculiarity of Mr Curran's wit, that even when it took the form of a play on words, it acquired dignity from the vein of imagery that accompanied it. Every jest was a metaphor. But the great charm and power of Mr Curran's eloquence lay in its fervour. It was by this that he animated his friends, and appalled his enemies; and the admiration which he thus excited was the child and the brother of love. It was impossible that a man whose mind was thus constituted, should not be a patriot; and certainly no man in modern times ever loved his country more passionately, than Mr Curran loved Ireland. The services he sought to render her were coeval with his first appearance before the public, and an earnest desire for her advantage and happiness attended him to his latest breath. The same sincere and earnest heart attended Mr Curran through all his attachments. He was constant and unalterable in his preferences and friendship, public and private. He began his political life in the connection of Mr Fox and never swerved from it for a moment. Prosperity and adversity made no alternation in him. If he ever differed from that great man, it was that he sometimes thought his native country of Ireland was not sufficiently considered. There was nothing fickle of wavering in Mr Curran's election of mind. The man that from an enlightened judgment, and a true inspiration of feeling, he chose, he never cooled towards, and never deserted. Mr Curran had has foibles and his faults, which of us has not? At this awful moment it becomes us to dwell on his excellencies. And as his life has been illustrious, and will leave a trait of glory behind, this is the part of him that every man of a pure mind will choose to contemplate. We may any of us have his faults: it is his excellencies that we would wish, for the sake of human nature, to excite every man to copy in proportion to his ability to do so.

Morning Chronicle, 16 October 1817 (R42)

No arrangements are yet made for the funeral of that lamented character, John Philpot Curran. Many of his friends wish the body to be conveyed to the sister kingdom; but this is opposed by others. He died worth only 30,000/ which is bequeathed to his natural children, viz two sons. His legitimate children were all, previously to his demise, amply provided for (*Morning Post*, 29 October 1817). Yesterday the mortal remains of the Right Hon John Philpot Curran were removed from Amelia-place, Brompton, for interment at Paddington Church. The funeral procession was quite unostentatious, consisting only of a hearse and four mourning coaches. The body was deposited, about seven, in one of the vaults under the Church' (*Morning Post,* 5 November 1817). One morning at an inn in the South of Ireland, a gentleman travelling upon mercantile business, came running down stairs a few minutes before the appearance of the stage coach, in which he had taken a seat for Dublin. Seeing an ugly little fellow leaning against a door post, with dirty face and shabby clothes, he hailed him and ordered him to brush his coat. The operation proceeded rather slowly, the impatient traveller cursed the lazy valet for an idle, good-for-nothing dog, and threatened him with corporal punishment on the spot, if he did not make haste and finish his job well, before the arrival of the coach. Terror seemed to produce its effect; the fellow brushed the coat and then the trousers, with great diligence and was rewarded with sixpence which he received with a low bow. The gentleman went to the bar and paid his bill, just as the expected vehicle reached the door. Upon getting inside, guess his astonishment to find his friend, the quondam waiter, seated snugly in one corner, with all the look of a person well used to comfort. After two or three hurried glances, to be sure that his eyes did not deceive him, he commenced a confused apology for his blunder, condemning his own rashness and stupidity; but he was speedily interrupted by the other exclaiming – "oh never mind – make no apologies – these are hard times, and it is well to earn a trifle in an honest way. I am much obliged for your handsome fee for so small a job – my name, Sir, is John Philpot Curran – pray what is yours?". The other was thunderstruck by the idea of such an introduction; but the drollery of Curran soon overcame his confusion; and the traveller never rejoiced less at the termination of a long journey, than when he beheld the distant spires of Dublin glitter in the light of a setting sun. This deserves to be recorded among the many comical adventures into which Curran was led by his total inattention to personal appearance (*Belfast Newsletter*, 29 August 1828).

On Thursday the mortal remains of the late Right Hon John Philpot Curran arrived in the Shannon steamer and were thence borne to Lyons, to be deposited for the present in the mausoleum of the Right Hon Lord Cloncurry, friend and political colleague of the illustrious dead. The removal was attended by the son of the deceased, W Curran Esq and M J O'Kelly Esq. Curran's remains have been brought over from England with a view to the re-interment in the Catholic cemetery of Glasnevin. The committee of the cemetery are erecting a splendid monument to his memory. To render the public funeral as striking and effective as possible it is not intended to inter the body in the cemetery until the approach of Term, when the members of the Bar and the representatives of the Irish people will be in town to attend it' (*Morning Post*, 28 July 1835). 'A committee for erecting a testimonial to the memory of the late Right Hon John Philpot Curran over the vault in the cemetery at Prospect, near Glasnevin, where the remains of this eminent Irishman, having been removed from England, are now interred [progresses]' (*Freeman's Journal* 25 May 1838). 'Died at Edinburgh, Cpt J B H Curran, second son of Right Hon John Philpot Curran' (*Belfast News Letter*, 21 Aug 1832). 'On the 18th December at her residence, 6 Mortimer-street, Cavendish-square, Sarah, widow of the Right Hon John Philpot Curran, some time Master of the Rolls in Ireland, at the advanced age of 89 years' (*Morning Post*, 25 December 1844). 'Died on 11th inst, at his residence, Argyll House, King's-road, Chelsea, after a protracted illness, Richard Curran Esq, eldest son of the late John Philpot Curran' (*Morning Post*, 15 Dec 1846). 'Mr W H Curran, late one of the Commissioners of the Insolvent Court, died on Tuesday week at his residence in Dublin. He was son of the late celebrated John Philpot Curran, Master of the Rolls' (*The Examiner*, 4 September 1858).

DAY, Judge Robert (1745/6-1841) Son of Rev John Day of Lohercannon House, Tralee and Lucy Fitzgerald, husband of (1) Mary Potts and (2) Mary Fitzgerald, father of Elizabeth (married Sir Edward Denny) and Rev John Robert Fitzgerald and Rev Edward Fitzgerald

'THE GOOD old judge', as in the language of popular affection we have been accustomed to hear him spoken of, is no more. The venerable ex-Judge Day died yesterday after a short illness at his residence in Loughlinstown House at the advanced age of 95 years. The kind relative, the true and steadfast friend, the benefactor of the poor, and the refuge of the distressed and the afflicted has at length given up his spirit into the hands of the judge of all flesh. It is not for us to attempt to do adequate justice to the many virtues of a character ever regulated by genuine Christian principles and whose heart was the chosen abode of the most exalted philanthropy. Of his character as a judge of the bench for many years, the history of his country will speak. His decisions were those of justice tempered by mercy and many a trembling wretch was rescued by that mercy from an ignominious death and reserved for repentance and forgiveness. As a kind, indulgent landlord, none stood higher in the estimation of the public, or in the affection of his tenantry who, with his highly respectable and numerous friends, will never cease to revere his memory. The painful event, which it has been our duty to record, took place on Monday last, at his seat at Loughlinstown House, near Dublin. The deceased was in the 97th year of his age. The *Evening Packet* of yesterday thus speaks of the deceased: 'He retired from the Bench, of which he was a conspicuous member, in 1819, having served his country in that capacity upwards of twenty one years. He was a contemporary of Chief Justice Downes and Justice Bradstreet. Before going to the bar he sat for a Fellowship and, though unsuccessful, his answering was of a respectable order. In politics he was a Whig of the old, but not of the modern, school. His latter years were employed in compiling a history of England, and translating the Lives of the Fathers of the Church with a view to posthumous publication. It is expected by his friends that he has left many valuable papers, which will be published. Frequently of late he had expressed his regret that he had not written a history of his own time, which would have covered the period of 97 years.' He was twice married. By his first wife he had issue one daughter, who married Sir Denny but by his second wife, whom he married very late in life, he had no issue. He was a most affable and pleasing companion, full of anecdote and of manners most gentle and condescending. By the poor of his neighbourhood his loss will be sorely felt. 'Large was his bounty, and his soul sincere'. During the last thirty years he was a constant resident at Loughlinstown, with only a short interval when he made a continental trip. Besides his pension he had a large fortune in the county of Kerry and he is supposed to have died rich. He has left a widow, a sister, and numerous relatives, to whom it is supposed, he has bequeathed his wealth. Of him it may be truly said, 'he never made an enemy, never lost a friend'. The late Judge Day has left the bulk of his fortune to the sons of his second wife, the Messrs Fitzgerald; to one his landed estate, said to produce an income of 4000*l* a year and to the other funded property estimated at 60,000*l*. It is said that some time previous to his death he offered to leave his estate to his grandson, young Denny, provided he would assume the name of Day, and that the young gentleman, having taken time to consider, peremptorily refused to change his name.

Extracted from *Freeman's Journal*, Feb 10 1841; *Kerry Evening Post* February 10 1841; *The Morning Chronicle*, Feb 16 1841; *The Standard,* March 1 & 11 1841 A biographical note on the Day family can be found in *Killarney Sketches* at www.lulu.com. This is a reproduction of a mid-nineteenth century publication by the son of Judge Day, John Robert Fitzgerald Day, with footnotes. (R24)

DICKENS, Charles (1812-1870)

THE LATE Charles Dickens. Mr Dickens was not only a successful author. No hearer of his readings could doubt that he had faculties which would have led to similar success in other pursuits. As an amateur actor he was, perhaps, almost without an equal, and even his reading of his own writings gave evidence of his wonderful power of impersonation. He was also an admirable and effective speaker, excelling in that peculiarly difficult form of eloquence which is appropriate to festive occasions. He was probably the best after-dinner speaker in England. The last public dinner over which he presided was the News-venders' Benevolent and Provident Institution. Thus it happened that to the last he showed himself the friend of literature in its lowest grade as well as a hard worker in its highest. At gatherings of this kind Mr Dickens was sure to set the table in a roar. He had a language and a method of his own which were inimitable, and he will be deeply and sincerely regretted by many benevolent societies to whom his services were rarely refused, notwithstanding the great pressure on his time. His capacity for business was as great as his power of speech and of writing; in fact, he was a clear-headed, prompt, vigorous man, of pure feelings and lively sympathies, who used his great powers under a sense of responsibility for the public good. He leaves a literary example which will be of lasting value to the morals and literature of his country. The circumstances of Mr Dickens's death, so far as they are at present known, may be briefly stated. He left London on the 1st of June, apparently in his usual health. On Wednesday evening last, when at dinner, Mr Dickens was seized with paralysis. Dr Steele, of Strood, Rochester, who has attended the family for many years, was sent for, and remained with him till nearly midnight. Dr Beard, of Welbeck-street, was telegraphed for from London, and arrived accompanied by Mr Dickens's eldest son; but it was apparent from the first that there was little hope of recovery. Mr Dickens had, we understand, been ailing for some time past, but during the week he visited Rochester and other places in the neighbourhood. Mr Dickens married early in life the daughter of Mr George Hogarth, who was for some years the musical critic of the *Daily News*. By this lady, who survives him, he had several children. Of two daughters, one is unmarried; the other is the wife of Mr Charles Collins, the son of the celebrated painter, and the brother of Mr Wilkie Collins, and himself an author and artist of ability. Mr Dickens's eldest son, Mr Charles Dickens, has been for some time the acting editor of 'All the Year Round'; another son is an officer in the army; and a third is a student in Trinity-hall, Cambridge.

Kerry Evening Post, 15 June 1870 (R41)

DOWNING McCarthy, Mr (1814-1879)

THE FUNERAL of Mr McCarthy Downing is fixed to take place at one o'clock tomorrow. His remains were removed to the Cathedral at Skibbereen this evening, whence the funeral will start at one o'clock for the family burial place at Caheragh, a distance of about seven miles from the town where his father, mother, and five of his family are interred. Up to the day before his death he retained full possession of his physical and mental powers. On that day he arranged his temporal affairs, and made a most edifying preparation for his end. Mr McCarthy Downing was son of Mr Eugene Downing, of Kenmare, and was the second of a family of three sons, including himself and two daughters. He was born in April 1814. In the year 1830, at the early age of 16, he was apprenticed to his brother as a solicitor and in 1835 he received his certificate admitting him to the profession. At about this time an incident occurred. Lord Musgrave, the then Viceroy, having been down in Killarney on a visit to Lord Kenmare, it was determined to present him with an address. The deputation, of which the Downing brothers and Mr Matthews, a liberal-minded Protestant clergyman of the town, were members, having presented the address returned to Kenmare, much pleased with the reception they got and adjourned to the hotel to celebrate it with a dinner.

Dining together in the same room in the hotel were also Lord Adam Loftus and a Mr Godfrey. The address was the principal topic of conversation and the references made to it so irritated Lord Loftus, who was bitterly opposed to its presentation, it drew from him some uncomplimentary allusions to the religion of the majority of those present. Young Downing demanded an apology; it was refused, and resulted in a challenge to a duel. The spot selected was the Priest's Level within a short distance of Kenmare and here the two disputants met but although the ground was measured, and the pistols loaded, through the intervention of Mr James Hickson, agent for Lord Lansdowne, the honour of both gentlemen was satisfied and the deadly encounter avoided. Mr Timothy Sullivan, of Prospect, near Kenmare was to have acted as Mr Downing's friend and MR William Mahony of the Point, Kenmare, to have discharged similar office for Lord Loftus. In the year 1836 Mr Downing removed to Skibbereen and the year following, at the age of 23, married Miss Jane McCarthy, daughter of Mr Daniel McCarthy of Dromore and the result of the union was a family of four sons and three daughters, all of whom, with the exception of one, survived. It was when O'Connell was rousing to action the dormant energies of the nation that McCarthy Downing made his first appearance on the Irish political platform. He did not identify himself with any party in the forty-night movement, but when that collapsed he helped two of its members who sought refuge in the west of the county Cork to escape to France. These were James Stephens and Michael Doheny.

Edited from *Freeman's Journal*, 12 January 1879 (R78)

EGAN, John (1784-1871)

PALLIDA MORS has at last knocked at the gate of No 1 Denny-street, and struck his waiting but unerring dart into all that was mortal of one of our oldest residents – John Egan Esq – whose name and symbol, as an apothecary, has adorned the walls of the Mall of Tralee for the best part of the present century, and whose sign of a golden 'Pestle and Mortar' was elevated over his door, on the Mall, with the well-known legend 'Kerry Medical Hall' long before the' old Castle of Tralee' fell a victim to the siege of the 'Crowbar brigade' of 1827. Mr Egan, better known by the familiar soubriquet of 'Johnny Egan' was a gentleman of no ordinary talents of a certain stamp. He was a clever practitioner, and he was the originator, author or inventor of the celebrated disease of the 'Emporium'. This calls to my recollection Johnny giving evidence in an insurance case before Judge Jackson, and examined by Mr Clarke (then a young sarcastic barrister on this circuit) when this disease was briefed to him, and when he (Clarke) thought he had a 'Griffin' in Johnny; but Johnny turned the tables on his examiner, and brought the laughter of

the whole court in thunder against Clarke, who, finding
he had caught a tartar, let the witness off the table,
highly complimented by 'Old Bandon Bridge' for the skill
and cleverness of his diagnosis. Mr Egan had also a
talent for the guinea trade and accumulated a large
fortune, but he has left no near relative either to mourn
his loss, or to thank him for the munificence of his
bequests. I understand he has left a large sum for the
relief of the poor of the town, where he made his money.
Mr Egan, in troubleous times, filled the office of
Chairman of the Town Commissioners, and by his
cleverness and monetary policy, did his fellow-citizens
good service – and worked them through very heavy
financial difficulties. Mr Egan was in early life a merry
boon companion, and has been for many years the
survivor of all his contemporaries – Frank Mack,
Stephen Walsh, Frank Healy, John Casey, 'et hoc
genus omnes' of the times. I never heard he was 'a
brother of the Mystic tie'. Mr Egan was also – "tis 60
years since' – a great admirer of the histrionic art, and
was an intimate acquaintance of Clarke and Lacey,
when they were successively the popular managers of
the 'old play house' in Chapel Lane and all of whom
have long since played their parts. Amongst those
companies he spent many an evening; but never made
his debut as an amateur behind the foot lights. He was
also an admirer of the stars of the companies; and he
used to tell some humorous stories of his adventures
amongst the 'gay Lotharios' of Tralee at that time. In
this theatrical society he acquired the taste for poetry
and rhyming that he indulged in until the curtain of this
world's stage dropt on him the 14th May 1871 at the
green old age of eighty-seven. He was a near relative of

the late Bishop Egan of Killarney for whose memory he had the greatest esteem. His 'dispensatory' and original 'formula' will be of great value to the whole profession, and I am sure that some of our rising embryo medicos will be found to edit them and bring them through the press for the benefit of medical science and to make a name for himself, on the great skill and knowledge acquired by the long experience of our lamented townsman. Mr Egan used to boast of his great skill as a 'chemist' and of having had the mantle of his uncle, Dr Sheehy, descend to himself in many voluminous volumes of Materia-Medica. On whom will the mantle of our old friend descend? Mr Egan was the father of the seed trade in Kerry, and wee do I recollect the cardboard bill on his shop windows, 'New Garden Seeds' printed in large coarse letters, and all illuminated by a village artist by daubing round the capitals a border of rose pink and yellow ochre in grotesque shadings and which was replaced there every spring to acquaint his customers of the fresh arrivals of his stock. Well do I recollect his shop supplied all the grand gardens from Tarbert to Ballybog, 'Tempora Mutantur'. His monopoly was broken in upon by Patt Sullivan, a qualified gardener bred to the trade, who served his time under the tutelage of Mr Forbes, the well-known gardener of Ballyheigue Castle in the days of old Colonel Crosbie. Patt afterwards worked in the Royal Garden at Kew Palace and was an intimate acquaintance of old George the Third. Then came Fennessy, a Limerick man who lived in Denny-street and who established a garden and nursery in Mr Wilson's garden where the corn market now stands. He was followed about the year 1839 by Robert Walpole, and from thence the progress of the seed trade can be easily traced to the several first class seedsmen of the present day in our town. But this is digression. We shall miss his statue at 'the corner' and his poetical greeting in the market place. We never shall look upon his like again. His home and his generation are alike, extinguished.

Kerry Evening Post, 17 May 1871 (R39)

FINN, Thomas (Royal Victoria Hotel, Killarney)

MR TIMOTHY Horgan of Coolick, County Kerry, has bequeathed to the Most Rev Dr Moriarty, Bishop of Kerry, 100l to be applied to such charitable purposes as he may deem desirable. Mr Michael Kearney, of Killarney, same county, has also bequeathed to his lordship 200l for the completion of the altar of the new church, besides 100l to the Convent of Mercy, Killarney. Mr Thomas Finn, of the Victoria Hotel, Killarney, has bequeathed 150l towards the completion of the new Catholic cathedral, Killarney, through the same eminent divine.

Freeman's Journal, 12 December 1861 (R34)

FITZGERALD, Sir Peter George (1808-1880)

SIR PETER George FitzGerald, of Glanleam, Valentia, and Ballinruddery, Listowel, both in the county of Kerry, commonly known as the Knight of Kerry, being the seventeenth in succession of his family who had borne that distinction, died at his residence at Valentia on Saturday last, after a long and painful illness, at the age of 72. The deceased baronet, the first of the house, was the eldest surviving son of the late Right Hon Maurice FitzGerald, of Glanleam, sixteenth Knight of Kerry, and many years MP for county Kerry, by his union with Maria, daughter of the late Right Hon David La Touche, of Marlay, county Dublin. Born in the year 1808, he succeeded to the family honours on the death of his father in 1849. He married in 1838 Miss Julia Hussey, daughter of Mr Peter Bodkin Hussey, of Farrinikilla House, Co Kerry, by whom he had a numerous family. He was a magistrate and deputy lieutenant for the county of Kerry, of which county he was High Sheriff in 1849; he was on the roll for High Sheriff of the county of

Carlow in 1875, and was also formerly deputy vice treasurer of Ireland. Sir Peter FitzGerald, as a resident landlord, always took an active part in all that concerned the prosperity of Ireland, and was especially known for the interest which he took in the success of the Atlantic cables, which it will be remembered are joined to a massive shore cable, drawn up the cliff at Foilhuinmerum Bay to the telegraph house at the top, not far distant from the beautiful country seat of the Knight of Kerry. Here at Glanleam he was honoured by visits from the Dukes of Edinburgh and Connaught, and also from the Prince of Wales. A few weeks since, her Majesty was pleased to confer a baronetcy upon him, but at that time he was unfortunately suffering from the illness which has now terminated fatally. He is succeeded by his eldest son, Mr Maurice (now Sir Maurice) FitzGerald, who was born in 1844, and entered the army, by purchase, as an ensign in the Rifle Brigade in March 1863, and became a lieutenant in February 1867, with which rank he served throughout the second phase of the Ashantee war from December 17 1873, as aide-de-camp to Sir Archibald Alison, taking part in the battle of Amoaful, the attack and capture of Beequah, the battle of Ardahan, and the capture of Coomassie. He was several times mentioned in the home despatches, received the medal with clasp, and was promoted to the rank of captain in April 1875. At the present time he is equerry to the Duke of Connaught.

Daily News, 9 August 1880 (R45)

FITZMAURICE, Major-General John (1793-1865)

FITZMAURICE, Major-General John, third son of John
Fitzmaurice and Mary Bourke, grandson of John
Fitzmaurice of Duagh and Margaret Stack (nee
Fitzgerald, Knights of Kerry), husband of Frances Maria
Watkins and father of Maurice Henry and John Gerald
We have to announce the death of Major-General John
Fitzmaurice, K.H., lieutenant of Her Majesty's Body
Guard, who died on Christmas Eve at Drayton Green,
Ealing. The late gallant officer, who had for some years
held the post of lieutenant of Her Majesty's Body Guard
(Yeomen of the Guard), entered the army in April 1811
as a volunteer in the Rifle Brigade, with which gallant
corps he served in the Peninsula till the end of the war
in 1814. He took part and was present at the action of

Sabugal, the battle of Fuentes d'Onor and the sieges and assaults of Ciudad Rodrigo and Badajos, at which latter he had a leg broken; also in the action at San Milan and the battle of Vittoria; skirmishing in advance he there, with two riflemen, took the first gun captured that day, and secured seven prisoners, pursuing the enemy to Pampeluna. He was present at the battles of Nivelle and Nive, together with those near Bayonne on 10th, 11th and 13th December 1813; the brilliant action with Soult's rearguard at Tarbes, and the battle of Toulouse, besides numerous minor affairs. He served also in the campaign of 1815, and led the advanced guard at Quatre Bras, where he was severely wounded in the thigh. In recognition of his distinguished military services he was made by His Majesty William IV, a Knight of the Royal Hanoverian Guelphic Order in 1833. His commissions bore date as follows: Ensign, April 25th 1811; lieutenant, Jan 14th 1813; captain, June 16th 1825; major, March 30th 1832; lieutenant colonel, Nov 9th 1846; colonel, June 20th 1834; and major-general, May 7th 1861. The gallant officer, on gaining his majority, went on half-pay. He had received a silver war medal with eight clasps for his services in the Peninsula, and the Waterloo medal. Major General Fitzmaurice was in his 73rd year. Note: Ulick, the eldest brother of Major-General John Fitzmaurice, is the great grandfather of playwright George Fitzmaurice of Listowel, who was involved in the Irish dramatic movement.

Published in the *Morning Post*, December 28th 1865. Article courtesy Eileen Chamberlain (R18)

FROUDE, James Anthony (1818-1894)

WE REGRET to announce the death of the well-known
historian, Mr J A Froude, which occurred at half past six
on Saturday morning at Salcombe, Devon. He was
unconscious for twenty-four hours before his death,
which was very peaceful. His illness dates back to June
last, when the fatigue caused by the delivery of a series
of lectures on Erasmus proved too severe a strain upon
his constitution. Liver trouble supervened, and for some
time before his death no hope was entertained of his

recovery. James Anthony Froude, youngest son of the late Venerable R H Froude, Archdeacon of Totnes, born in Dartington, Devonshire April 23 1818, was educated at Westminster and at Oriel College, Oxford, where he graduated in 1840, taking a second class in classics, and he proceeded MA in due course. In 1842 he became a Fellow of Exeter College and at the time of his death held the office of Professor of Modern History at Oxford University. He was ordained a deacon in the Church of England in 1844. His 'Nemesis of Faith' appeared in 1848, and reached a second edition in the following year. This marked his defection from the teaching of the Church of England. About this time Mr Froude resigned his Fellowship, and he was obliged to give up an appointment which he had received to a teachership in Tasmania. In 1856 he published the first two volumes of his *History of England from the Fall of Wolsey in the Defeat of the Spanish Armada* which has been continued from time to time; Vols 11 and 12 having been published in 1870, concluding the work. One of the most marked features of the work is an elaborate attempt to vindicate the reputation of Henry VIII. His *Short Stories on Great Subjects* appeared in 1867, being reprints of essays which had appeared in various periodicals, Mr Froude was installed Rector of the University of St Andrews March 23 1869 on which occasion the degree of LLD was conferred upon him,. On September 21 he executed a deed of relinquishment of the office of deacon. In the autumn of 1872 Mr Froude went to the United States where he delivered a series of lectures on the relations between England and Ireland The burden of his addresses was that Irishmen had themselves, to a large extent, caused their country's prostration by their own intestine jealousies and want of patriotism. An animated controversy ensued between him and Father Thomas Burke, the Dominican orator. At the close of the year 1874 Mr Froude was sent by the Earl of Carnarvon, Secretary of State for the Colonies, to the Cape of Good Hope, to make enquiries respecting the late Cadre insurrection, and he returned to London in March 1875. His later works are *The English in Ireland in the Eighteenth Century*, three vols, 1871-74, *Caesar; A Sketch*, 1879, and *Reminiscences of the High Church Revival*. Having been appointed executor to Thomas Carlyle, he published his *Reminiscences*, two vols, 1881, and the first part of his biography, *Thomas Carlyle, a history of the first forty years of his life*, 1882, and *Reminiscences of his Irish Journey in 1849*, London 1882. *Oceana* was published in 1886, an account of Froude's voyage to Australia and elsewhere. In 1883 he published *The English in the West Indies or The Bow of Ulysses;* in 1889, *The Two Chiefs of Dunboy, an Irish romance of the last century*; in 1890, a *Life of Lord Beaconsfield*; and, recently, a *Life of Erasmus*. In his biographical sketch of the deceased historian, the *St James Gazette* sums up his adventures as follows: 'As a yachtsman, a keen and expert angler (in which capacity he was a frequent visitor at the Bedford Arms, near Chenies, in Buckinghamshire) and as an excellent though quiet talker, Froude will be remembered by a number of intimate friends and admirers. But to the world at large, he was known exclusively by his books. Many will estimate him from an acquaintance with the four volumes of Short Studies alone among his writings. Nor need an estimate so formed be an erroneous one for these brilliant essays contain, in epitome, much that is valuable and most suggestive in Froude's philosophy. Whether as a pure critic, or as a knights-errant in defence of national prejudice, or a teller of parables (who that has read can ever forget his essay on a railway siding?) he equally enlists our sympathies and delights us by the lucidity and sincerity of his style. His frequently emotional interpretation of history may lead people to compare him with Charles Kingsley (with whom, as also with Professor Max Miller and the late Lord Sydney Godolphin Osborne, he was connected by marriage) and with J L Motley; but certainly, in so far as literary faculty is concerned, Froude is greater than either. With his death the English-speaking world has to deplore the loss of one of the great contemporary masters of modern English prose'.

North Eastern Gazette, 3 December 1894 (R75)

Froude was a frequent visitor to Kerry, and spent summers at Derreen House near Kenmare. One of those experiences is told in *Muckross, A True Story of Love on the Lakes during the Famine* at www.lulu.com. See also his description of a Kerry murder in *An Rabach of Cummeengeera: the fact and the theatre,* published at www.lulu.com and a Cork murder, *Dunboy, The Murder of John Puxley* at www.lulu.com

GANDSEY, John (c1767-1857), piper, father of John

DEATH of the eminent piper, John Gansey (*sic*). This venerable old man, whose name and whose song have been associated for over half a century, with the talismanic recollections of Killarney, in the breasts of millions at home and abroad, is no more. He passed away calmly and peacefully on Thursday last, at Killarney, believed to be in the 90th year of his age. Healthy and genial to the last, his white hairs streaming in bardlike amplitude down his neck, no later than Little Christmas Eve, we heard him discourse the plaintive airs of our country with unimpaired effect, and 'lilt' the *Modereen Ruagh*, with as much sportive energy as when his noble patron, the late lamented Lord Headley, called forth the soul of the minstrel.

Kerry Evening Post, 7 February 1857 (R25)

GANDSEY, John

SUDDEN DEATH JULY 1848 – John Gansey (*sic*), when on his way on Saturday evening from Killarney to Aghadoe where he resides, suddenly dropped dead. He had been ailing since his return about three weeks ago from America where he and his father, the celebrated piper minstrel, had been for the last year and a half on a professional tour. On the evening in question he was seized with a fit of coughing and in ten minutes after was a corpse (*Examiner*).

Kerry Evening Post, 22 July 1848

A biographical note on Gandsey is contained in *Killarney Sketches* at www.lulu.com. This is a reproduction of a mid-nineteenth century work, with footnotes.

GASCOIGNE, Thomas Oliver (Died 24 April 1842)

IT IS OUR painful duty to record the sudden death of Thomas Oliver Gascoigne, Esq, the eldest son of Richard Oliver Gascoigne Esq of Parlington near Aberford in this county. A few weeks ago, the unfortunate gentleman left Parlington for London, being then in a poor state of health. In London, his health improved much and he contemplated an early return to the beautiful scenery of his native home. That return however has been effected in his coffin. It appears that on Sunday last, about noon, he unexpectedly breathed his last, at his lodgings in London. He had told his valet to go down and get his dinner, as he was not wanted. The valet did so, and returned to him about two o'clock when he found him sitting on the floor, with his head leaning against his chair, quite dead. Mr J Moody, surgeon, considered his death was caused by apoplexy. It further appeared that the deceased, who on the demise of his father would have come into possession of £60,000 a year, was subject to epilepsy. Verdict – Died by the visitation of God. We understand that the remains were brought down by railway to Parlington for interment at Aberford, being the first of the family that has not been interred at Barwick-in-Elmes.

Edited from *York Herald*, 30 April 1842 (R79)

GASCOIGNE, Richard Oliver (Died Dec 1842)

THE SUDDEN death of Richard Oliver Gascoigne, the direct
male heir of this ancient family, on Wednesday last, has
produced a sensation in the neighbourhood of Leeds, little
inferior to that which was occasioned by the death of the only
son of the late Sir Thomas Gascoigne, who met his fate by an
accident in hunting and expired at Walling Wells, the seat of
Sir Thomas White, Notts, in 1809 at the age of 24 years. On
the death of his father, Sir Thomas Gascoigne, on 11th
November in the following year, Richard Oliver Esq
succeeded to his princely possessions in the West Riding of
Yorkshire and in Ireland, and in compliance with the will of Sir
Thomas, took the name of Gascoigne. Thomas Charles
Gascoigne, the eldest son of Mr Oliver Gascoigne, of
Parlington, died some years ago, leaving only one brother
Richard, who is now dead, and two sisters, Isabella and
Elizabeth, who survive him. This family is descended from the
intrepid Sir William Gascoigne of Gawthorpe in this county,
Lord Chief Justice of England who was interred at Harewood
in the year 1412. The most celebrated instance of his
authority was the committal to prison of the Prince of Wales,
afterwards Henry V. The Gascoignes intermarried with the
Wentworth family in the 17th century and Sir Thomas
Wentworth, Earl of Strafford, was a descendant of that union.
Edited from *Morning Post*, 2 January 1843

GASCOIGNE, Richard Oliver (Died April 1843)

ON SATURDAY last at Weymouth, where he had gone for the benefit of his health, Richard Oliver Gascoigne Esq of Parlington in the West Riding. The sudden deaths of his two sons, in the short space of a few months, had a powerful effect upon the mind of Mr Gascoigne and cast a gloom over every domestic scene of the family residence. This partly induced him to visit Weymouth, where he sickened and died at an advanced age. He has left two daughters to mourn their loss and we understand that, owing to the death of the two sons, the family estate will go to Earl Fitzwilliam.

Morning Post, 25 April 1843

More genealogy in Recovery of Estates case, Hungate v Gascoigne, *Hull Packet*, 12 April 1831. Oliver Estate history in *Castle Oliver & the Oliver Gascoignes* by Nicholas Browne at www.lulu.com

GEORGE, Private

AT 11 o'clock on Thursday morning the remains of
Private George, 1st Batt Royal Fusiliers, who was killed
in the Headford Junction ambush, were removed from
the military barracks to the new cemetery for interment.
The funeral procession was headed by a firing party,
followed by the regimental band, after which came a gun
carriage with the coffin draped in the Union jack. The
whole battalion marched in the procession, the rere
being brought up by a force of police under Capt
Lancaster, DI. Very Rev Canon Madden, Killarney,
officiated at the graveside. At the conclusion of the
burial service three volleys were fired and the Last Post
sounded.

The Kerryman, 2 April 1921 (R73)

GRIFFIN, Gerald (1803-1840) Native of Cork

DIED of Typhus fever, on Friday, at the North
Monastery, Cork, Gerald Griffin Esq, late of this city,
author of The Collegians, Tales of the Munster Festivals
and other works of high literary merit. Mr Griffin was
born in the city of Limerick in the year 1803. His genius
manifested itself very early in life and at the early age of
nineteen he proceeded to London for the purpose of
commencing his literary career as an author, but he
soon became alarmed at his own celebrity and as the
piety by which he was characterised became every day
more fervent and absorbing, he resolved on abandoning
his literary pursuits and devoting himself exclusively to
the service of religion. He was still induced to continue
contributions to the press but with such repugnance of
feeling, such a fear of the danger of literary ambition, as
to impede the free exercise of his powers and to deprive

his latter works of the vigour and charm of his earlier productions. Yesterday, immediately previous to the funeral, a solemn High Mass for the dead was chanted in the chapel of the monastery at which the Very Rev M B O'Shea officiated as high priest attended by the Rev Messrs Crowe and Hayes as deacon and sub-deacon, and the Rev D Foley as master of the ceremonies. About the hour of twelve o'clock the funeral train commenced to issue from the monastery, and although it did not pass beyond the immediate precincts and it rained heavily during the time, the crowds that attended furnished a consoling evidence of the worth which endeared. On reaching the small grave yard of the monastery, where the body was deposited by the sides of those who had laboured and died in the same field of charity, a beautiful and touching panegyric on the deceased was pronounced by the Very Rev M B O'Shea.

Edited from *Manchester Times*, June 20 1840 & *Freeman's Journal*, 25 June 1840 (R37). Griffin's two-volume *The Collegians* is said to have formed the basis for Boucicault's play, The Colleen Bawn, which dramatized the alleged murder of Ellen Hanley in Co Clare in 1819. See note at entry Michael John WHITTY for an earlier version of events which has been reproduced with footnotes.

HARRINGTON, Thomas

THE FUNERAL of Mr Thomas Harrington, London sub-editor of the *Freeman's Journal* took place yesterday. At half-past one o'clock the cortege which started from Addergown for Killury churchyard, the family burial ground, was a large and imposing one, and strikingly testified to the esteem and respect with which the deceased young pressman was held by the people of his native place. The line of cars reached close on two miles, and to the graveyard a distance of over five miles, the coffin was borne on the shoulders of friends. Wreaths were presented from his colleagues on the London staff of the Freeman's Journal, bearing the inscription 'As a token of love and esteem' and from the reporting staff of both Houses of Parliament with a similar inscription. Wreaths also came from the nuns of the Presentation Convent, Lixnaw; Mr and Mrs Harrington, Tralee, and from Mr T Galvin and family, Tralee. The bier was covered also with numerous floral crosses and emblems. Among those who attended the funeral from Tralee were: Mr T Lyons, TC; Mr and Mrs E

Harrington, Kerry Sentinel; D J O'Rearden, solicitor; B O C Horgan, solicitor; W J Galvin, T Gibson, W J Poyntz, J Griffin, F Walsh, A Raymond, Kerry Evening Post; R H Greene, Cork Herald; J Quinnell, Kerry Weekly Reporter; J Roche, Newcastle West; J Fitzgerald, J McEnery, T McEnery, M Walsh, M Cremins, T Studdert, Kerry Sentinell (sic); T O'Leary, E Brosnon (sic), T Healy, E Stack, W Galvin, T McEnery, T McMahon, P Cashman, Ballyheigue; R Cussen, R Boyle, JP, Listowel; J Walsh. A striking feature in the cortege was the marching in processional order of a body of young men numbering over 300 immediately behind the coffin. They came from the parishes of Kilmoiley, Ballyduff, Causeway, Lixnaw, and Abbeydorney, and all wore mourning emblems.

Freeman's Journal, 19 December 1893 (R43)

HARTLAND, Henry Albert (1840-1893)

THE DEATH is announced of the well-known water-colour painter, Henry Albert Hartland, the melancholy tidings having been telegraphed to his brother, Mr William Baylor Hartland. The artist was a native of Mallow, being the youngest son of the late William Baylor Hartland of Bellevue, near that town, and was born on 2nd August 1840. He was educated chiefly in Cork, and was a distinguished pupil of the School of Art. His talents were early evinced, and he had not long emerged from pupillage before he acquired that admirable style which had made his works so popular. There was in them evidence of knowledge and remarkable skill, but their chief attraction lay in the loving appreciation of natural beauties which fitted him to be their interpreter. He was also a lover of the gentle craft. After a period of earnest and varied work, and when his reputation had been well established here, in cork, Mr Hartland went to Liverpool where his merits were immediately recognised, and where many of his pictures realised large prices.

Freeman's Journal, 30 November 1893 (R44)

Among the 'Sale of 130 of Albert Hartland's water-colour pictures at auction by Messrs Walker and Ackerley, at the Law Association Rooms, Cook-street: Threshing Corn; Sunset Isle of Wight; Old Shroeham Brighton; Sunset Bamridge; A Gloomy Evening; Near Barmouth; On the Mersey; Glengariffe Church; A Stormy Day; Glengariffe; Arthog; After Rain – Welsh river; Lough Ina Connemara; Arthog Moor; On the Moor Arthog; A Lake in Mayo; Near Llandudno; A Misty Day on Shore; A Welsh Tollgate; Hay Making, Capel Curig; Near Castlebar, Mayo; A Wet Day ot Ogwen; A Showery Day, Lough Ina; A Storm on the Coast; Gathering Turf, Mayo; From Shanklin; Conway Falls; At Steep Hill Cove; The Way over the Moor; The Flood; A Study of Ferns; At Castlebar; A Mountain Lake; Glengariffe; Autumn; Pensarn; On the Road, Cwm Bychan; Fog clearing away Barmouth; A Grey Day; A Mountain Torrent; Arthog; Hay-making, Mayo; Eagle's Nest Killarney; After the Rain; Shanklin Chine; Autumn Tints; Plantation, Arthog; Sandhills, Barmouth; Bog, near Shannon Bridge (Liverpool Mercury, 14 May 1881). 'At the Southport Spring Exhibition 'Killarney' realised £27 6s, Albert Hartland' (*Liverpool Mercury*, 10 June 1889). ''Killarney' a beautiful water colour picture by Mr Hartland realised £36 15s at Messrs Eddison and Taylor, auctioneers, High Street' (*Huddersfield Daily Chronicle*, 12 Oct 1893)

HAYES, Angelo (1820-1877)

ALTHOUGH for some reason, not explained to the
public, our Dublin Academy has not been opened to
visitors until more than two months after the usual time,
and when many of its former frequenters have either
gone to the country or to some of the many watering
places that woo their sojourn there during this hot
weather, yet more than an average attendance crowd
daily this fashionable resort. Indeed, rarely have the
ancient walls of the Academy been covered with
paintings more attractive to visitors than those there at

present. It is most gratifying to see, year after, year, the progress of our Irish artists onwards and upwards. Many of the paintings by Messrs Marquis, Duffy, Falconer, &c, might challenge competition with any living landscape painters in Europe, while Catterson Smith stands unrivalled as a portrait painter. Many of your readers may remember to have seen in the Academy a few years since a cabinet painting of Sir Dominic Corrigan in his study, and hundreds who had seen it pronounced it to be one of the most perfect gems in portrait painting they had ever beheld. Angelo Hayes still likes the 'Soldier Laddies', of which he is so faithful a delineator. 'Preparing for the Day's March', no 65 and 'The Deserter' no 351 are fair specimens of his skill in what may be said to be his peculiar department, while his 'Glena Cottage, Killarney' no 318 exhibits him as a lover of nature, and no careless delineator of one of its most lovely scenes.

Freeman's Journal, 12 August 1866 (R57)

HEADLEY, Lady (1776-1863) Anne Matthews, wife of
2nd Lord Headley, Charles Winn Allanson (1784-1840)

A DARK and gloomy cloud has gathered around the
sunny hills of Aghadoe, and has spread its sombre
shades not only over the distant mountains of
Castleisland and Abbeyfeale, but also over the peaceful
'happy valley' of Rossbeigh. The large-hearted, ever
open-handed Lady Headley is no more. Full of love –
for she had attained, we are informed, her ninety-
seventh year – and amidst the deep-felt sorrow and
lamentations of her numerous and well cared

dependants, the 'Good Woman' – as her tenants loved to call her – expired at an early hour on Monday morning at Aghadoe House, the family mansion, near Killarney. The affliction caused by the death of this truly noble lady is not confined to the tenantry on the Headley estate. Many a poor pensioner on her bounty in the town of Castleisland will mourn the parental hand now cold in death. In Killarney too, there is wide-spread sorrow, for she not only spent her money there, but 'when winter cold brought Christmas old', its poor, as well as those of her more immediate vicinity, were not forgotten. Indeed, as late as last Christmas, four bullocks, sold to the victuallers of Killarney, were re-purchased by her ladyship, by the pound at the full market price, and disposed of as a portion of her accustomed charities at that holy season. A beautiful anecdote which we heard from the lips of a tenant on her estate may find a place here. On the occasion of one of Lady Headley's visits to a portion of the estate, where she was always hailed with a blessing, an aged tenant said, 'God bless your Ladyship, you are always doing us good here, we would like to have you doing us good when you're in heaven'. 'How is that?' asked Lady Headley, much amused. 'By giving us leases'. And not only were leases granted, but the rent fixed by two trusty and experienced valuators. The extensive and well-regulated estates, of which her ladyship enjoyed a life use, and which was managed by her excellent and highly-respected agent, Mr Talbot, with so much mutual advantage to proprietor and tenantry, now reverts to Lord Headley, who since his accession to the title has generally resided at Brighton. The mortal remains of the venerable and ever to be lamented Lady Headley were this morning deposited in the family vault immediately adjoining the chancel window of the new parish church at Aghadoe, besides those of the late Lord whom she survived twenty years. The outer coffin was massive oak, carved with rich Genoa crimson velvet, and ornamented with elaborately wrought mountings, laid on with great taste and judgment – the whole presenting a gorgeous piece of workmanship, highly creditable to Mr Justin McCarthy and to the workmen engaged by him in its execution. The chief mourners were the Right Hon Lord Headley and his brother the Hon Rowland Winn. Her ladyship's numerous and respectable staff of domestics, male and female, all attired in deep mourning, were also in attendance. The general cortege was numerous and highly respectable, and comprised all ranks, creeds and classes from different parts of the country. Amongst the nobility, gentry and clergy whom I recognised as present or in some few unavoidable instances, amply represented by their agents and equipages, were Lord Viscount Castlerosse, MP, Right Hon H A Herbert, MP, The McGillycuddy of the Reeks, DL, Sir Wm D Godfrey, Bart, and Mr Charles Godfrey; Right Rev Dr Moriarty RC, Bishop of Kerry, and Ven Archdeacon O'Leary, John M Bernard, DL, D C Coltsmann, DL, Thomas Gallwey, JP, D S Lawlor, JP, Daniel Mahony, JP, Dunloe Castle; Henry Leahy, JP, Edward Rae, JP, Keel; James O'Connell, JP, and sons; Francis Bland &c &c and the neighbouring clergy of all persuasions with scarce an exception. There was also a vast number of the trading and farming classes, and a large number of the medical and other professions from distant parts of the country, including Dr Crumpe, Tralee; Major Drew, 75th Regiment; William John Neligan, &c. At the entrance to the church-yard the procession was met by the rector of the parish, Venerable Archdeacon Bland, and his curate, the Rev John Westroppe Brady, both fully robed in ecclesiastical costume, who preceded the remains into the church. The pulpit, reading desk and communion table, were appropriately draped with the sombre memorials of the deepest sorrow, in the midst of which the sublime and impressive service of the Established Church was commenced, and having been concluded to the entrance to the vault the remains of the benevolent and bountiful 'good woman' were lowered into the final resting place amidst the unrestrained wailings and lamentations of hundreds, many of whom will long remember the generosity of their *flaghool ban maugh*'.

Extracted from *The Kerry Evening Post*, 18 & 28 February 1863 (R28). A biographical note on Lady Headley can be found in *Killarney Sketches* at www.lulu.com. This is a reproduction of a mid-nineteenth century publication, with footnotes.

HERBERT, Rev Arthur (1783-1835)

ON WEDNSEDAY morning last, the Rev Arthur Herbert of Cahernane House, near Killarney, Rector of the Union of Castleisland, accompanied by Robert Hickson Esq, eldest son of John Hickson Esq of the Grove, took his seat on an outside car for Tralee. They were proceeding on their way from Killarney when, coming down the hill near Farranford turn-pike, the harness was broken and the splash-board pressed upon the horse, which, after plunging for several minutes, dashed off at full speed. The Rev Gentleman, it would appear, considering himself in a perilous situation, leaped off the vehicle and came heavily on the side of his head and shoulder – after the fall, he got up – said he was severely hurt in the head – walked some distance to a cottage on the road, leaning on Mr Hickson's arm – he complained of his limbs and sight becoming weak, and gradually got into a state of insensibility with stertorous breathing. Medical assistance was at once sent for to Castleisland, Killarney, and Tralee – neither bruise or mark of any kind could be perceived on the head, but the right side of the hat and top of the right shoulder of his coat showed evidently that the lamented gentleman fell with great violence on the right side of the head – he was largely blooded without relief, and as the last resource and the only remedy from which relief could in any possibility be rationally expected for removing the extravasation of blood which evidently was the cause of pressure on the brain. Doctor Crumpe at once made room the trephine, under the temporal muscle of the right side over the middle artery – on having performed the operation, blood, as was expected, was found extravasated on the membranes of the brain, but unfortunately in that general way which completely debarred the accessibility of success from an operation, which under other circumstances has been known occasionally to take place – the symptoms increasing, the lamented gentleman expired in 14 hours after the accident occurred. Few, very few, even of the illustrious house of Herbert, has ever been conveyed to the silent earth with feelings of more widely spread sorrow, more intense regret than will be he whose death it has been our melancholy duty to lay before our readers. It is not alone in the circle of his own fire-side, and hospitable board; it is not alone among persons of his own high class or creed that his death has created such unmingled regret. There is not one within the whole range of our county, whatever may be his grade in society, or even amid the angry politics of the day – to whatever party he may be attached, who has not heard of his melancholy end with deep and heart-felt regret, or who will not long cherish the memory of the warm-hearted man, the urbane and unaffected gentleman, the benevolent and charitable Christian. A Coroners inquest was held on his remains at Flesk Cottage on Thursday, and the usual verdict of Accidental death returned by the jury.

Obituary from *The Kerry Evening Post*, 25 July 1835 (R14) Note: a sketch of the Herbert family of Cahernane can be found in *The Herberts of Currans & Cahernane* at www.lulu.com. Rev Herbert's clerical record is contained in *The Church of Ireland in Co Kerry, a record of church and clergy in the nineteenth century* available to download at www.lulu.com

HERBERT, Henry Arthur (1815-1866) Son of Charles John Herbert and Louisa Anne Middleton, husband of Mary Balfour and father of Eleanor, Henry Arthur, Charles and Blanche

THE SAD duty has devolved upon us this evening of announcing the death of the Right Hon Henry Arthur Herbert of Muckross, senior representative and Lieutenant of this county. This melancholy event took place at eight o'clock on Monday evening at Adare Manor, the seat of the Earl of Dunraven where the deceased gentleman, accompanied by Mrs and the Misses Herbert, had been staying for a few days previous. The family of the deceased gentleman is of old and high position in this county, and is lineally descended from Sir William Herbert, Knighted by Henry the Fifth and forms a branch of the Powis Herberts. Colonel Herbert was born in 1815 and early left a minor. He was educated at Cambridge. He served the office of High Sheriff of this county the year after he attained his majority. In 1837 he was married to Mary, daughter of James Balfour Esq of Whittingham in Haddingtonshire. Colonel Herbert was returned for this county at the General Election in 1847 as a Conservative and without a contest. He shortly after became a Liberal Conservative or Peelite to which shade of political opinions he has since adhered. At every election since he was re-elected and always without opposition. A singularly handsome man, Ramohun Roy declared he was one of the finest men he had seen in Europe. A pleasing speaker, he was a consistent supporter of the late Lord Palmerston by whom he was selected in June 1857 to fill the onerous and responsible office of Chief Secretary for Ireland which office he held till the accession of the Derby Ministry in March 1858. He was made a Privy Councillor in 1857 and had the Lieutenancy of the County conferred upon him in 1853 and also the Colonelcy of the County Regiment. In 1861 he had the honour of entertaining the Queen, Prince Consort and other members of the Royal family at Muckross on the occasion of their visit to the Killarney lakes. As a country gentleman Colonel Herbert was most active in the discharge of the several duties of a Grand Juror, Justice of the Peace, and Poor Law Guardian. The best proofs that can be given as to the manner in which he discharged his duties as a landlord are to be seen in the comfortable tenantry and well cultivated farms that are to be found on all his property. Colonel Herbert has left four children, two sons and two daughters. His eldest son, by whom he will be succeeded in his estates, is Captain Henry Arthur Herbert of the Coldstream Guards. We may remark that Colonel Herbert's father died comparatively young and in Mallow, where he had gone for the benefit of the waters, which were reputed to have some medicinal virtue. Before eleven o'clock on Tuesday a large concourse of people had already assembled in front of Muckross House waiting to pay a last compliment to a gentleman who had filled so large and influential a space in Kerry history during the past quarter of a century; leading gentry of the centre and north of the county travelled by the 10 o'clock train from Tralee arrived at Muckross. Refreshments and a hot cup of coffey (sic) was laid on in the dining-room for all who wished to partake of them. At half past 11 o'clock the coffin, a most beautiful one, covered with crimson cloth, was borne from the door of Muckross House on a bier on the shoulders of the tenantry, immediately followed by six chief mourners – Captain Herbert, the Earl of Dunraven, Colonel Long, Charles Balfour Esq, Hon Vesey Dawson MP and Herbert Stewart Esq – on through the demesne, and passing by the old Abbey was carried into that gem of a church built by the deceased gentleman in the village of Cloghereen – the immense funeral cortege following on foot. On arriving at the church, which was most tastefully dressed in black, the coffin was taken in and followed by as many as the building could accommodate. The service was most impressively performed by Rev C E Wright, chaplain, assisted by the Rev William Wade, curate of

Killarney. On the removal of the coffin from the church, the Dead March in Saul was feelingly performed on the harmonium before the coffin was conveyed into the old graveyard of Killeagy and there interred in a temporary vault. Though the very unseasonable inclemency of the weather in the morning – a continued fall of snow with which the country was covered – kept at home very many who had made preparations to be present, the funeral was very large.

Extracted from *The Kerry Evening Post* February 28 & March 3, 7 & 10 1866 (R23). The Herberts of Muckross form the subject of James Anthony Froude's *Muckross, a True Story of Love on the Lakes during the Famine* and is available at www.lulu.com

HERBERT, Admiral Sir Thomas (1787-1861) Son of
Richard Townsend Herbert of Cahernane, and brother
of Rev Arthur Herbert of Cahernane (see R14)

A TELEGRAM was received in Killarney on Monday
afternoon announcing the death of distinguished naval
officer Admiral Sir Thomas Herbert KCB at 1 o'clock pm
on Sunday the 4th inst at his residence, Cadogan Place,
London. Sir Thomas Herbert was the second son of the
late Richard Townsend Herbert of Cahirnane House,
Killarney, Esq, and uncle of the present popular

proprietor of that romantic residence, the Rev Richard Herbert. His career in the navy was an exceedingly brilliant one. When in command of the Calliope, a 26-gun frigate, he was most successful in the capture of slavers[1], and when last afloat on board the Blenheim his gallant deeds before the walls of China were particularly distinguished. He represented the borough of Dartford for some years, from which he retired at the last election. During the time that he occupied a seat in the House of Commons he was invariably the consistent supporter of the Conservative leader. By his death a large accession of landed property reverts to the Right Hon Colonel Herbert, MP, his life being the Last in several old leases on the Muckross estate – it was insured to a considerable amount in different offices by different parties. There is now only one surviving brother of this large and highly respectable family, viz, Lieut-Colonel Charles Herbert, at present in command of Her Majesty's 54th Regiment. The late Admiral was in his 74th year, unmarried, and, it is said, in possession of wealth to a very large amount.[2]

Obituary published in *The Kerry Evening Post*, August 7, 1861 (R17)

[1] slaver = ship or person involved in slave trade
[2] This article suggests Sir Thomas was born circa 1787, and not 1793, as indicated in some sources

HICKSON, Mary Agnes (1825-1899)

WE REGRET to have to record the loss of a distinguished Irish antiquary and a member of this Club, Miss Mary Agnes Hickson, who died at Mitchelstown on the 6th April, at the age of 73 years. She was the daughter of the late Mr John James Hickson, Solicitor, of Tralee, who was connected by marriage and descent with many of the Elizabethan families of Kerry. She was a woman of undoubted talents, and the labours of her life may be said to have been almost entirely devoted to the study of the history and topography of her native county. Her opinions on some of the events in the chequered history of this island were not such as a perfectly unbiased historian (if such there be) could agree with; but this is not the time, or the place, to inquire into them. Her learned inquiries into our ancient records, and her valuable contributions to historic literature will always remain worthy of the highest praise. She was buried in the new cemetery, Tralee.

Journal of the Limerick Field Club, Vol 1, No 3, 1899, p40
(R62)

'It will interest Irish readers to learn that Mr J A Froude is
writing a preface for a new work now in the press
relating to the so-called massacre of Protestants in
Ireland in 1641. The volume will consist of a selection
from certain 'depositions' now lying the library of Trinity
College, Dublin. In dealing with this congenial subject
Mr Froude is sure to display all that delicate regard for
the truth and that fine perception of historical impartiality
which marked his previous writings upon the same
subject, and with such a veracious and unprejudiced
colleague as Miss Mary Hickson (who is to write the
introductory part of the work), he will no doubt send forth
a very plausible justification of the absurd views which
now prevail in certain anti-Catholic circles in regard to
this misrepresented episode in Irish history' (*Freeman's
Journal*, 8 January 1884).

HUSSEY, Samuel Murray (c1825-1913) Son of Peter
Bodkin Hussey and husband of Julia Agnes Hickson of
The Grove, Dingle

THE DEATH of Mr Samuel Murray Hussey took place
on Saturday night at his residence, Aghadoe House,
Killarney. The deceased gentleman, who was in his
89th year, was the oldest magistrate in Kerry and the
best known of Irish land agents. Among a number of
landed proprietors whom he represented were the Earl
of Kenmare, Lord Headley, Sir George Colthurst and Sir

Edward Denny. The late Mr Hussey may be said to have borne a charmed life. Few men in Ireland have been made the recipients of so many threatening letters, and fewer still perhaps, have had so many attempts made upon their lives. 'Threatened men, however, live long' and the truth of this has been singularly exemplified by Mr Hussey's experiences. How little effect these repeated threats and the many attempts made to give practical effect to them have had upon him is shown by the fact that he has died peacefully in his bed. In 1904 Mr Hussey, then in his 80th year, was induced to publish Reminiscences of an Irish Land Agent, a view of life as it impressed itself on 'the most abused man in Ireland'. He adopted farming as a profession after his school days; he learned farming in Scotland, and returned to Kerry with the intention of farming on the scientific method he had learned. He found the land in Kerry so subdivided that it was impossible to obtain a farm of sufficient extent and so migrated to Cork to become assistant land agent to his brother-in-law, the Knight of Kerry, agent to Sir George Colthurst. This became the business of his life, he at one time received the rents of one-fifth of the whole county of Kerry. As the outward and visible sign of the distant or absentee landlords, he obtained the greater share of the hatred felt for the latter. Perhaps the greatest example of this was the attempt to blow up his house at Edenburn, Tralee in 1884. The remains of Mr Hussey were removed from Aghadoe House to Killarney Railway station this morning, accompanied by a considerable number of neighbouring residents and the principal residents of the town, where the coffin was entrained for Tralee. At Tralee, a big assemblage of people awaited the arrival and accompanied the removal to Dingle railway station. There, a special was in waiting to convey the cortege to Dingle. The station at Dingle was crowded with local people who joined the procession to the church; a large concourse of mourners assembled at the different towns through which the remains were taken. The service was celebrated by the Bishop of Limerick and Ardfert following which the coffin was taken to the family vault for interment.

Extracted from *The Kerry Evening Post*, 12 November 1913 and *The Killarney Echo*, 15 November 1913 (R26)

IRON, Edith Margaret (1914-1986) Daughter of Walter Valentine Knowles and Elizabeth English (nee Everitt) Died at St Christopher's Hospice, Sydenham on 8 March 1986 and was cremated at Falconwood Crematorium, London

EDITH MARGARET was my maternal grandmother. She never spoke much about her family but it is believed she was one of three children (brother 'Ginger' who died relatively young and sister Betty) when she met and married Ernest Victor Iron while working as a chambermaid in a London hotel where he was a porter. She married on 1st March 1938 in black for her father, Walter Valentine Knowles, was killed by a lorry as he stepped off a tram shortly before her wedding. (Her mother seems not to have married Walter Knowles, for her name was Elizabeth English, nee Everitt. Edith had an assortment of older half/step siblings about whom nothing is known.) Edith's new husband went away to war in 1939, leaving Edith with two young children and not returning until the war was over in 1945 (my grandfather had six medals to show for it, including the African, Italian and Indian stars). At that time my uncle Christopher was conceived, some six years younger than his brother and my mother, Doreen. My grandmother loved gardening, my memories of her are her visits on Saturdays by bus to spend the day planting flowers and weeding. She was the happiest of souls, accompanied me on my first job interviews in London, an area she knew well having worked in the city for many years as a messenger for the Ministry of Defence. She loved charity shops, and would arrive at our house with 'presents' which to a teenager was embarrassing but no doubt from her my own love of the shops was born. I used to wait with my nan at the bus stop and longed for the day I could drive and take her home in style; I eventually passed my test at age 20 and it gave me the greatest pleasure to have my nan by my side to drive her to her door. In later life she lived at Tivoli Gardens, Woolwich but before that it was somewhere in Bermondsey, a block of flats that had a concrete playground with a concrete ship outside where we played; I liked staying there and playing with her big black telephone or counting the number of train carriages that passed on the railway track from the window at the back of her flat. She was divorced in late life, the separation of war took its toll on her relationship and my grandparents parted quite late in life. My grandfather, a bus conductor on the number 36 Peckham route, who used to give us the odd ends of paper till rolls if we happened to board, re-married, and became a step-father to a young family in Peckham but this did not deter my nan from keeping his letters to her under her pillow until the day she died, sadly of cancer in St Christopher's Hospice in Sydenham. Short in stature but graceful and every inch a lady, Edith was big hearted and so much loved. She wanted to live to her 90s, to live longer than her own mother. I only wish she had.

Composed 28 September 2010 by Janet Murphy, granddaughter (R2)

JELLETT, John Hewitt (1817-1888) Son of Rev Morgan Jellett (rector of Grean, Co Limerick and Tullycorbet, Co Monaghan) and Harriett Townsend Poole of Mayfield, Bandon, Co Cork

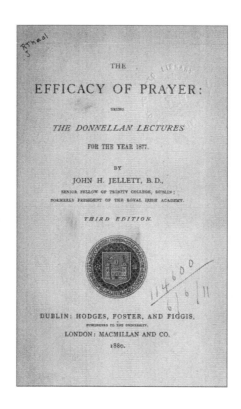

THE REGRET with which we announce the death of the Rev John Hewitt Jellett, BD, Provost of Trinity College, will be shared by all who ever had the pleasure of coming in contact with him. The sad event was entirely unexpected. A few days ago Dr Jellett caught a cold, such as is common in weather like the present;

yesterday alarming symptoms were manifested and about eight o'clock the end came. On Christmas Day last he had completed his seventieth year, but the brisk, firm step was that of a man who preserved in age much of the vigour of youth, and the slight bend in his figure was the stoop of the life-long student, not the droop of an enfeebled form. Born at Cashel in 1817, he entered Trinity College whilst little more than a boy, and after a distinguished course was elected a Fellow in 1840. Thenceforth, his career was associated with the College. In 1848 he was appointed Professor of Natural Philosophy, and two years later his treatise on the Calculus of Variations won for him an honoured place in the first rank of contemporary mathematicians. Numerous papers on Pure and Applied Mathematics followed, all distinguished by marked ability, notably his contributions to the study of Experimental Optics, and his notes on the application of mathematics to chemistry. Many of these essays were published in the Transaction of the Royal Irish Academy of which body Dr Jellett was elected President in 1869; others appeared in the Journal de Mathematiques; and some in the Proceedings of the British Association. Other studies shared his industry. His Essay on Some of the Moral Difficulties of the Old Testament which appeared in 1867, claimed general attention. In the following year he was appointed by the Crown a Commissioner of National Education, and in 1872 his opus magnum, the Treatise on the Theory of Friction was published. With the exception of some fugitive papers on scientific subjects, and various sermons, his next work was the book on The Efficacy of Prayer in 1878. A few months afterwards he was co-opted to fill the vacancy on the

Senior Board created by the death of Dr Luby, and when in 1881 the Provostship was rendered vacant through the demise of the late Dr Humphrey Lloyd, the Crown chose Dr Jellett as his successor. Personally estimable in all the relations of life, the late Provost was a special favourite with the students, by whom he was held in the greatest respect, and wherever graduates of 'Old TCD' are to be found, the news of his death will excite sincere sorrow.

Freeman's Journal, 20 February 1888 (R53)   Chief mourners at his funeral on 23 February 1888: Captain Jellett, RA; Mr Jellett, BL; Mr H H Jellett, sons of the deceased; the Very Rev Dr Jellett, Archdeacon of Cloyne, and Mr Sergeant Jellett, brothers; the Rev Canon Morgan Jellett, Rev A G Fitzpatrick, and Professor Fitzgerald.

KELLY, Mother Teresa

DEATH OF Rev Mother Teresa Kelly, Presentation
Convent, Listowel – A long life of activity, intelligence
and holiness under trying circumstances, endeared
Reverend Mother Teresa Kelly to all who knew her
personally or by report. Upwards of fifty years ago Miss
Kelly entered the Presentation Convent, Killarney and
soon after passing through an edifying novitiate was
appointed superioress. In this important office she
distinguished herself by her prudence and zeal alike; her
charity knew no limit and yet she never involved her

community in embarrassments. During her term of office in Killarney, the first of the monks of La Trappe, whose abbey is now so well known at Mount Melleray, near Cappoquin, came to this country from France. They were penniless and depended for support on the charity of the people. The first of those who stretched out the hand to help them was the Rev Mother Teresa. Her influence procured them a house to live in, and her pecuniary aid to their establishment in Ireland was important. Visitors to the abbey of Mount Melleray may hear of a lady who is publicly prayed for by the monks as a great benefactress to their order, well known to the older brothers – this lady is Mother Teresa. All, but a few old monks on crutches, have died, of the brothers who came over from France, and as silence is one of the chief disciplines of La Trappe, few of the present community know the name of the lady for whom the public prayers are offered. Having filled with honour the office of superioress at Killarney for several years, Mother Teresa, with a few sisters, left the community to found a convent at Milltown, a small town at the bend of Dingle Bay. Under her able government this undertaking prospered, and the schools attached were filled with the children of the peasantry and townspeople. Here Mother Teresa remained until she had passed her fiftieth year. At this period of life few men or women undertake new and important works, but Mother Teresa, hearing of the great want of educational establishments in North Kerry, consented to break her attachments to the convent she had founded and made prosperous, and begin anew in Listowel. She founded the convent of Holy Cross in that town upwards of twenty years ago, with three assistant sisters. Of her acts of charity during the famine years no praise could be too loud. She was the chief reliance of priests and people in that district during that dreary period. Her small community gradually gained accessions, and on the day of her death she had the happiness to see it one of the most prosperous and beloved of the presentation convents. Many priests on the foreign and home missions owe the means which enabled them to prosecute their studies to this holy woman, and would regret her loss were they not sure that she has passed to a place where the virtues she practised and the peace she loved and taught here are eternal.

Freeman's Journal, 26 October 1864 (R35)

KITCHENER, Lord (1850-1916)

Among Herculean deeds, the miracle
That mass'd the labour of ten years in one
Shall be thy monument. Thy work is done
Ere we could thank thee, and the high sea swell
Surgeth unheeding where thy proud ship fell,
By the lone Orkneys, ere the set of sun.
Robert Bridges, Poet Laureate, 1916

THE SECRETARY of the Admiral announces that the
following telegram has been received from the
Commander-in-Chief of the Grand Fleet: 'At 10.30
British summer time, morning, I have to report with deep
regret that his Majesty's ship Hampshire (Capt Herbert J
Savill, RN) with Lord Kitchener and his staff on board,

was sunk last night about 8pm to the west of the Orkneys either by a mine or a torpedo. Four boats were seen by observers on the shore to leave the ship. The wind was north north-west, and heavy seas running. Patrol vessels and destroyers at once proceeded to the spot, and a party was sent along the coast to search, but only some bodies and a capsized boat have been found up to the present. As the whole shore has been searched from the seaward, I greatly fear that there is little hope of there being any survivors. No report has yet been received from the search party on shore. HMS Hampshire was on her way to Russia. HMS Hampshire was an armoured cruiser of the county class, of 10,850 tons. The vessel was built at Elswich and was completed in 1905. The total estimated cost of the ship including guns, according to Brassey's Naval Annual was £856,527. Her principal armament consisted of four 7.5 inch and twenty 3 pounders. She carried a complement of 655 men. The special party consisted of Lord Kitchener with Lieut-Col O A Fitzgerald, CMG (personal military secretary), brigadier-General W Eillershaw, Second Lieut R P MacPherson, 8th Cameron Highlanders, Mr H J O'Beirne, CVO, CB, of the Foreign Office, and Sir H F Donaldson, KCB, and Mr L S Robertson of the Ministry of Munitions, Mr L C Rix, shorthand clerk, Detective MacLaughlin of Scotland Yard and four personal servants. Henry Surguy Shields, Walter Gurney and Driver D C Brown, RHA, were also attached to the party. Lord Kitchener was the third child of the late Colonel Henry Kitchener, who came to Kerry after the famine of 1847. Colonel Kitchener was a friend of the late Mr Pierce Mahony of Kilmorna, who lent him Gunsborough Villa, about three miles from Listowel, on the road to Ballylongford, where on the 24th June 1850, Lord Kitchener was born. He was baptised on the 22nd September 1850 at Ahavallin Church, by the late Rev Robert Sandes. In or about this date Col Kitchener bought an outlying portion of the Knight of Glin's estate, which he afterwards sold and purchased Crotto, near Kilflynn, about seven miles from Tralee, from the late Mr Samuel Julian, where the Kitchener family resided for several years and where Lord Kitchener spent his boyhood. Thus Kerry has every right to claim Lord Kitchener as her son, and to take special pride in his glorious career which has ended so tragically in the service of the Empire. His last visit to Kerry was in August 1912, when he spent some days in Tralee and visited the scenes where he spent his youth.

The Kerry Evening Post, 7 June 1916 (R52)

The nation mourns this week as it would never have mourned for a man who mere 'got things done'. Lord Kitchener had personality. It is not a thing to be defined or accounted for. We see it in its effects…. Lord Kitchener was the people's man. When those who called for him turned on their idol the nation did not move. Its confidence was unshaken. At no moment could the critics lay any sort of claim to have the country behind them. The cult of Kitchener had given a distinctive colour to the passionate patriotism called forth by the war. The purist may protest, but to the man in the street the new army will be known as 'Kitchener's Army'.' (Extracted from *The Kerry Evening Post*, 10 June 1916)   Speaking at Klugerdorf tonight, Sir Abe

Bailey said, 'Just before I left England I asked Lord Kitchener how things were going. Lord Kitchener replied, 'Well, the Germans are now in a much more serious position than people think, especially in the interior, and they remind me of a prize fighter who is staggering and dazed. If they give me what I want, I will give them the knock-out blow'.'. (*Kerry Evening Post*, 21 June 1916)   Lord Kitchener demises to the use of his first and other sons, with remainder to his first and other daughters with remainder to Commander Henry Franklin Chevallier Kitchener, RN, son of Henry Elliott Chevallier Kitchener [brother] … with remainder to Henry Hamilton Ktichener, son of General Sir Frederick Walter Kitchener [brother] …Among other legacies the deceased left £5,000 in trust to pay the income thereof to his half-sister, Letitia Henrietta Emma Karvara, for life, with remainder in equal shares to her children, on failure of issue to the holder of the title or dignity of Earl Kitchener of Khartoum. (Extract from Lord Kitchener's Will, *Kerry Evening Post*, 1 July 1916)   'Probably the most impressive scene witnessed here [New York] during the present war developed last night at the great Allied Bazaar now in progress in this city in honour of the memory of Lord Kitchener…Shouting and laughing at one minute to nine changed into a procession of mourners … motor cars were stopped and women in evening clothes bowed their heads side by side with the humblest of Britain's friends on the side walk when the bugle sounded. 20,000 faces turned towards the front of the great hall and 20,000 heads were bowed when the Rev Dr Manning, rector of the famous Trinity Church read short prayers in memory of England's war secretary … the New York crowd forgot to hide their emotion, and when the band played Onward Christian Soldiers, everyone took up the refrain like a mighty army'. (Extract from *Kerry Evening Post*, 1 July 1916) 'The Select Vestry of the Tralee Union of Parishes: a proposal has been made to raise funds to repair and restore the old parish church of Kilflynn as a fitting memorial to Lord Kitchener, who when a boy, resided in that parish and was an accustomed worshipper in the church'. (Extract from *The Kerry Evening Post*, 22 July 1916) It may be of interest to clergymen who are arranging memorial services for the late Lord Kitchener to know that a South African lady, with whom he was on very friendly terms during the Anglo Boer war (she was then a girl), managed to persuade him to fill up a page in her book of confessions. One of the questions was, 'What are your favourite hymns?'. Opposite this he wrote as follows: '27 Abide With Me; 73 God Moves in a mysterious way; 428 The Saints of God their conflict past; 437 For all the Saints who from their labours rest'. The numbers of course refer to Hymns, Ancient and Modern and it is perhaps typical of his unfailing grasp of detail that he should remember them'. (*The Kerry Evening Post*, 22 July 1916) Lieut-General Sir Frederick Kitchener, the youngest brother of Lord Kitchener and Governor and Commander-in-Chief of Bermuda, died last night after a short illness following an operation for appendicitis' (*Irish Independent*, 8 March 1912).

LEAHY, Henry (1820-1870) Son of John Leahy and
Elizabeth Ashe of South Hill, Killarney

WE REGRET to have to announce the demise on
yesterday morning at his residence Flesk, near
Killarney, after a tedious illness of Henry Leahy, Esq,
JP, in the prime of life. Mr Leahy succeeded over 20
years ago, on the death of his father, the late John
Leahy, Esq, JP, of Southill, to the agency of the
Muckross estates in this county, and by his kind and
judicious management of the vast interests entrusted to
his care, he succeeded in preserving the unwavering
affections of his principals and the respect and
attachment of one of the best circumstanced body of
tenantry in Ireland. As a magistrate, a grand juror, and a
poor law guardian, Mr Leahy's loss will long be deplored
by those with whom he was associated in public life; and
while amongst his own family and his numerous friends,
he will ever be remembered for the strength and
sincerity of his attachments; by the poor of his town and
neighbourhood, he will always be regretted as a large
handed and charitable benefactor.

Obituary from *The Kerry Evening Post*, 25 May 1870 (R10)
Note: a sketch of the Leahy family of South Hill can be found
in *The Herberts of Currans & Cahernane* at www.lulu.com

LEAHY, John (1770-1846) Married to Elizabeth Ashe (1789-1864) and had a large family

THE RESPECTED gentleman John Leahy Esq departed this life yesterday morning at his residence at South-hill near Killarney. Mr Leahy, who has been for some time past very feeble, had reached the advanced age of 75 years. During a long period Mr Leahy has occupied a prominent place in this county as agent to very extensive landed proprietors, including the Muckrus and Ardfert estates, and in that trying position he has secured for himself the confidence of his principals, the gratitude of the numerous tenantry over which he was placed, and the respect of the public. He was also an active and intelligent magistrate. In private life he was a warm and steadfast friend; and in his family circle he was beloved as an attached husband and kind parent.

Obituary from *The Kerry Evening Post*, 24 June 1846 (R9)
Note: a sketch of the Leahy family of South Hill can be found in *The Herberts of Currans & Cahernane* at www.lulu.com

LEAHY, John (1809-1874) Son of John Leahy and Elizabeth Ashe of South Hill, Killarney, and husband of Matilda Emma Leahy nee White of Shrubs, Co Dublin and father of John White Leahy

IT IS WITH extreme regret that we have to announce the sudden demise of the respected Chairman for this County, John Leahy Esq, QC, which sad event took place in Newcastle this morning. Nothing could have been more unexpected. The health of Mr Leahy has been of late very much improved and when opening the Sessions in this town on Friday last, his appearance gave no intimation that his career was soon about to be closed. On this morning as he was preparing to open the court in Rathkeale, exactly at eleven o'clock, he was stricken down almost instantaneously, and breathed his last without a groan. It is now ten years and a half since Mr Leahy was appointed to the Chairmanship, having opened his first session in the month of April 1864. During that period, no uneventful one, he has won one distinctive reputation – that characteristic which is most to be desired in a judge – unchallenged integrity. A deep reflective and painstaking lawyer, Mr Leahy's decisions were very seldom questioned, and bore unmistakable weight in the higher courts. In his untimely departure, this county is deprived of the services of an important law officer of the Crown, who dealt out justice irrespective of creed, class or of private feeling, and who never spared time or trouble when it was necessary to bestow upon a subject a more than usual amount of reflection and care. When the telegram reached South Hill, the residence of deceased, it was received by Mrs Leahy, her only son John having been at the Madame McGillycuddy's, at the Reeks, since the previous evening where he had been invited to dine. Today about 2 o'clock he proceeded through Killarney on his way home quite ignorant of the sad news that was to meet him on his arrival at his late father's mansion, with none to comfort him or console him but his bereaved mother, a lady much respected in Killarney and its neighbourhood. At the time the painful news was communicated to the Chairman at Quarter Sessions, a brother of the deceased, Mr Thomas Leahy, occupied a seat in the vicinity of the chairman when he apprised of the occurrence by his nephew, Mr John Richard Leahy, of the Flesk Mills.

Obituary from *The Kerry Evening Post*, 14 October 1874 (R11)   Note: a sketch of the Leahy family of South Hill can be found in *The Herberts of Currans & Cahernane* at www.lulu.com

LEAHY, John White (1852-1907) Son of John Leahy QC
and Matilda Emma White, husband of Agnes Caroline
Cole of Wingland Cottage, Norfolk

IT IS WITH the deepest regret we have to announce the
death of Mr John White Leahy, JP, DL, of South Hill,
Killarney, aged 55 years. He died suddenly of heart
failure on Friday, the 6th inst, at his own home. Mr
Leahy was educated at Eton and at University College,
Oxford. He read for the Bar, but never followed that
profession, for on his father's death, soon after he came
of age, he took up his permanent residence at Killarney.
As a young man he was an athlete, a keen sportsman,
and a good rider. At the age of 25 he became High
Sheriff of the county, and ever since has discharged a
variety of public duties. He was the senior magistrate –
senior in standing though not in years – at the Killarney
Petty Sessions, and it was on last Tuesday, September
3rd, that he presided at that court. His high principle

and strict impartiality of mind won for him the confidence of all classes in the community. As a landlord he remained on friendly terms with his tenants throughout the long agrarian struggle. But it was to temperance work that the main effort of his life was devoted, and in that field of reform no labour seemed to him too great. One particular point may be mentioned. I Ie would note down the names and addresses of those who were fined for drunkenness at Petty Sessions, and follow up each individual case with close and personal attention. In numberless other ways he was in a special sense the friend of the poor. His house was visited by all in the district who were in trouble; they sought advice from him and never failed to get good counsel. His unknown acts of kindness are recorded in the hearts of many Kerry peasants. He was a man of strong and deep religious convictions; his religion was, indeed, the inspiration of his life. He was a member of the Irish Church Synod, and it was he who started the annual gathering now known as the Killarney Convention. In October 1906, he married Agnes Caroline, daughter of Mr Thomas Elmer Cole, of Wingland Cottage, Norfolk. The place he occupied in this county was in certain respects a unique one; and even outside the large circle of his friends his memory will be cherished for his singleness of purpose and his whole-hearted devotion to his ideals.

Obituary from *The Kerry Evening Post*, 11 September 1907 (R13) Note: a sketch of the Leahy family of South Hill can be found in *The Herberts of Currans & Cahernane* at www.lulu.com

LEAHY, Matilda Emma (1829-1907) nee White, daughter of William White of Shrubs, Co Dublin, wife of John Leahy, QC, and mother of John White Leahy

N HER 78th year, widow of the late John Leahy QC, of South Hill, eldest daughter of the late William White Esq, of Shrubs, Co Dublin and grand-daughter of Mr Luke White, MP, of Woodlands, Co Dublin. In 1851 she married the late Mr John Leahy QC and the only child of the marriage was the late Mr John White Leahy. Five of her brothers sat with their father as members of the Reform Parliament at the same time. Her sisters became Mrs Fitz Herbert, Mrs Little and Mrs Law. For the past 56 years she has resided at South Hill, during which time she has earned the esteem and regard of all classes in the district by her goodness, amiability and benevolence. The remains were removed from her residence to Killeagy Cemetery, and the interment took place in the family vault. The cortege was extremely large and representative of all classes and creeds. Amongst those who sent wreaths were – her sorrowing daughter (in law), Colclough family, Constance Nash, Elner and Betty, her servants, Denis Hegarty and Katie Hegarty.

Obituary from *The Kerry Evening Post*, 21 September 1907 (R12)   Note: a sketch of the Leahy family of South Hill can be found in *The Herberts of Currans & Cahernane* at www.lulu.com

LE FANU, William Richard (1816-1894)

WILLIAM RICHARD LE FANU, second son of the Very
Rev Thomas Philip Le Fanu, LLD, Dean of Emly and
Rector of Abington, in the county of Limerick, was born
on 24th February 1816, at the Royal Hibernian Military
School, Dublin to which institution Dr Le Fanu was then
Chaplain. The eldest son was the well-known novelist,
Joseph Sheridan Le Fanu. William Richard Le Fanu was
educated at home, and afterwards entered Trinity
College, Dublin, graduating as BA of the University in
1839. He then became a pupil of Mr (afterwards Sir)
John MacNeill, under whom he was engaged on
extensive sea-reclamations, harbours, and other words.
With the development of the railway system Mr Le
Fanu's work took principally that direction. Sir John
MacNeill was Engineer-in-Chief of most of the principal

railways first constructed in Ireland: the Dublin and Drogheda, opened in 1844; the Dublin and Cashel, opened first to Carlow in 1846, then to Thurles in 1848, and finally completed to Cork under its present name of the Great Southern and Western Railway. During these years Mr Le Fanu and Mr Matthew Blakiston were Sir John MacNeill's principal assistants, the former having charge of all the Parliamentary and other work south of Dublin. In 1846 he acted as Resident Engineer in charge of the completion of the Cork terminal section of the Great Southern and Western Railway, and went to live at Rathpeacon House, near Cork. On the termination of Sir John MacNeill's connection with the Great Southern and Western Railway, Mr Le Fanu became the Consulting Engineer to that Company and under his advice and superintendence the branches and extensions to Killarney (and afterwards to Tralee), to Tullamore (and afterwards to Athlone), to Roscrea (and afterwards to Parsonstown and Nenagh), and from Mallow to Fermoy, were carried out. He also designed and carried out railways for other companies: the Limerick and Foynes line; the Bagnalstown and Ballywilliam; and the Dublin, Wicklow and Wexford Railway from Wicklow to Wexford. He was Consulting Engineer of the Cork and Bandon Railway Company, and in 1856 designed the extensions of that line, which were not then sanctioned by Parliament, but have since been carried out. In 1861 he also became Consulting Engineer to the Board which had charge of the lighthouses round the coast of Ireland, then called the 'Ballast Board', but now known as the 'Board of Irish Lights'. During the short time he was adviser to the Board no lighthouse work of any special character engaged his attention. In July 1863, Mr Le Fanu accepted the position of Commissioner of Public Works, then vacant by the retirement of Sir Richard Griffith. The change from active professional work, with the uncertainties, not in themselves uninteresting, with which the result of new projects are attended, was not at first much to Mr Le Fanu's taste; and he hesitated to give up the freedom of private practice with its more remunerative prizes, for the harness of a high Government official. Friends, however, strongly pressed him, and he became Second Commissioner, Colonel Sir John McKerlie, KCB, becoming the Chairman of the Board. From the time he assumed these duties he devoted himself wholly and thoroughly to the work of the department. The Board of Works for Ireland has entrusted to it business of a much wider nature than is indicated by the title of the department. Besides the charge of all Government and public buildings, it takes, in Ireland, the place of the Public Works Loan Commissioners, and to some extent that of the Inclosure Commissioners, in England. The Board is also charged with the maintenance of Inland Navigations, and the Commissioners are likewise members of the Board of Control for Lunatic Asylums, and Commissioners in charge of the harbours of Kingstown and Howth. It was therefore no sinecure to which Mr Le Fanu succeeded when he became a Commissioner of Public Works. All applications for Government loans for public works, landed property improvement, drainage of lands, erection of farmsteads, scotch-mills, planting, improvement in navigation and water-power, came under his control. He had also to hold all meetings for making awards under the Arterial Drainage Acts for assessing charges for improvements, and to advise as to all matters in connection with inland navigation, harbours and piers, fisheries, and post roads, which came under the control of the Board. All loans, sanctioned by the Local Government Board, which sanitary authorities sought to borrow from the Treasury, came under his supervision. Except during his annual holiday or on inspections he was hardly ever a day absent from the Office of Public Works, and by making a rule of never allowing arrears to accumulate, he got through a vast amount of steady work year by year. As a railway engineer Mr Le Fanu carried out many large and important works, though none were of such novel or striking importance as to call for special description. It is authoritatively stated that, so carefully were estimates prepared by him, that in no case was the amount exceeded which he advised as the capital to be provided. He was a well-known figure in the Committee Rooms while in private practice, no session passing without his having Bills to support or oppose. He was retired from the post of Commissioner of Public Works in 1890, under the age regulation then for the first time applied to the whole Civil Service. In 1893 he published his well-known memoirs entitled, 'Seventy Years of Irish Life'. Mr Le Fanu died on 8th September 1894 at his residence, Summerhill, Enniskerry, Co Wicklow, in the seventy-ninth year of his age. He was elected a Member of the Institution on 24the May 1853.

Published in *Journal of Institution of Civil Engineers* (ICE),Minutes of the Proceedings, Vol 119, Issue 1895, pp395 –397. ICE, One Great George Street, Westminster, London, SW1P 3AA. (R58)

Yesterday the remains of Wm R LeFanu were removed from his late residence, Summerhill, Enniskerry, to the local churchyard for interment. The great respect entertained for the deceased gentleman was testified in a marked degree by the attendance at the funeral. The line of carriages reached a long distance along the road from Summerhill towards the Dargle .... The massive oak coffin which was strewn with wreaths and floral crosses, bore the following inscription: 'WILLIAM RICHARD LEFANU, Born 24 Feb 1816, Died 8th September 1894'. At the special request of the working people of Enniskerry, the coffin was carried from Summerhill to the churchyard. The chief mourners were: Thos Philip LeFanu, Rev Fletcher LeFanu; William LeFanu, Brinsley LeFanu, Victor LeFanu, Henry LeFanu, Lieut Hugh LeFanu, RN, sons; George C May, A C May, Croker Barrington, Jellet Barrington, nephews; Col P F Robertson, J R D Robertson, nephews-in-law. (*Freeman's Journal*, 12 September 1894) NOTE: William Richard Le Fanu was married in Dublin to Henrietta Victorine Barrington on 15 January 1857 (she died 29 July 1899 at Summerhill) and his issue included daughters Charlotte and Emma (*Morning Post*, 4 March 1895).

LESLIE, James Blennerhassett (c1865-1952)

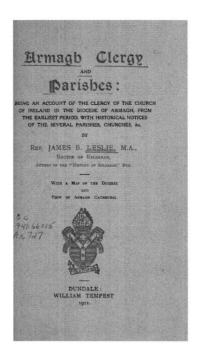

REV CANON James Blennerhasset Leslie, D.Litt, will today retire from the rectorship of Kilsaran, Co Louth, a position he has held for 52 years. He was born at Cloncannon, Co Kerry and first ministered in Belfast and Portadown (*Irish Independent*, 31 December 1951). Rev Canon J B Leslie, MA, DL, MRIA, who died at his home, Tigh Beg, Haddington Park, Glenageary, Co Dublin, aged 87, was a native of Clouncannon, Beaufort, Co Kerry. At Trinity College he won the Bishop Forster's Divinity Prize. He was curate at Christ Church, Belfast from 1891 to 1894 and at Portadown until 1899 when he was appointed rector of Kilsaran, Armagh, to which he remained attached until his retirement this year. He was appointed Prebendary of Mullabrack, Armagh in 1925, and became Chancellor of the Cathedral in 1934. In 1943, he was appointed Prebendary of Yagoe and Representative Canon of Armagh in St Patrick's Cathedral, Dublin. He was the author of a number of historical works. He was an uncle of Temple Lane, the author.

Irish Independent, 21 April 1952 (R54)

'Sir. The spectacle of Mr Francis Joseph Bigger attacking Primate Ussher is too good for words! A terrier worrying a dead lion is not in it. I think I know as much about him and his character, his intellectual abilities and attainments, and his attitude towards the Irish language as Mr Bigger, and I believe the attack made upon him in your paper unjust, uncalled for, offensive in expression to your readers who belong to the Church of Ireland, and extremely wanting in good taste....I would advise Mr Bigger to study a little more of Ussher's works, which he evidently criticises unread, or else, if he writes again on the subject, I suspect it will be his own and not Ussher's reputation that will suffer. When Mr Bigger's fame and name are forgotten, the fame and name of the great Irishman he belittles will still flourish. James B Leslie, Kilsaran Rectory, Castlebellingham, Co Louth'. (*Irish Independent*, 11 June 1912).

LEVER, Charles (1806-1861)

CHARLES LEVER – "Harry Lorrequer" – the Irish
novelist, who died at Spezzio a few weeks ago, was
born in Dublin on 31st August 1806. His father was a
builder of substance and respectability in the Irish
capital; and the future romancist having been at an early
age destined for the medical profession, studied with
that view, first in his native country, and afterwards in
France. When cholera for the first time made its
appearance in Ireland, Lever was selected as medical
officer of a district in the north, comprehending the city
of Londonderry and the towns of Coleraine and
Newtownlimavady; and his practice is stated to have
been wonderfully successful. He was subsequently
nominated physician to the Embassy at Brussels, and,

while occupying that position, made a brave dash at fame by publishing periodically "Harry Lorrequer," which, on its completion, he dedicated to Sir G Hamilton Seymour, then envoy at the Belgian Court. This story made Mr lever a literary celebrity, and he did not fail to pursue his success. "Harry Lorrequer," was followed, as time passed on, by "Charles O'Malley," "Jack Hinton," "The Commissioner," "Our Mess," "The O'Donoghue," "St Patricks Eve," "Roland Cashel," "The Knight of Gwynne," "The Daltons," "The Dodd Family Abroad," "The Fortunes of Glencoe," &c. Mr Lever's novels are characterized by Irish humour and exaggeration; and, although he has sufficiently proved his acquaintance with life on the Continent, whether the inhabitants are occupied with peace of war, he is generally considered most fascinating when the scene is laid in the "Green Isle." While engaged in the production of his numerous works of fiction, he, in 1842, took up his residence in the neighbourhood of his native city, and figured for a time as editor of the 'Dublin University Magazine.' This kind of work was, no doubt, found rather irksome by the dashing and brilliant Irish novelist. At all events, he returned to the Continent about 1845, and resided there, with short intervals of absence, up to the period of his death.

Dundee Courier, 16 June 1861 (r68)
Illustration from *Charles Lever His Life and His Letters* by Edmund Downey, Vol II, 1906

LEVEY, John

IT IS with regret that we have to record the death of Mr
John Levey, which sad event occurred with awful
suddenness on Thursday 17th inst, at his residence,
Seaforth, Liverpool. Mr Levey had been in his usual
health, and was engaged in literary work when he was
seized with paralysis. He rallied for an hour, but a
second stroke unhappily placed him beyond medical
aid. The deceased was the youngest son of Mr R M
Levy of Dublin, and brother to Paganini Redivivus and
Mr W C Levey. As a playwright and an author of
pantomime his name was a familiar one. He once
occupied a prominent position as an Irish character
actor, though of late years he has devoted himself
almost exclusively to pantomime work, and his was a
name to conjure within many of the Yorkshire and
Lancashire towns. He was at various times the lessee of
several provincial theatres. Mr Levey leaves a widow
and two children to mourn his loss. The interment took
place on Sunday last in the burial ground adjoining the
St Peter and St Paul's Catholic Chapel, Crosby. Among
the mourners were the widow, Mrs John Levey; eldest

son, Master John Levey; brother, Mr Edwin Evans; sister-in-law, Miss Amy Ambrosine; Mr and Mrs J W Lawrence, Thornton's Varieties, Leeds; Mr C R Brettell, Rotherham; Mr and Mrs David Graham, Mr John Atkinson, and Messrs Wm and James Graham, Theatre Royal, Dewsbury; Mr De Souza, Quartermaster Sergeant Chitland, Mrs Chitland, Mr and Mrs bond, Messrs A and E bond, Mr J W Law, Mr T Norris, Mr A Little, Mr A Stannyer, Mr Nono, Mr J Crook, and Mr Caine. The Rev Father Nixon officiated both in the chapel and at the grave side. The ceremony was a very impressive one, and was witnessed by a large concourse of people. The coffin was literally covered with floral offerings. The wreaths and crosses were from the following: Mr John Levey, Mr and Mrs J W Lawrence, Mr C R Brettell, Mr and Mrs Arthur Greasley, Mr and Mrs Graham, Mr Atkinson, Mr De Souza, Mr and Mrs Bond and Mrs Willsey.

The Era, 26 September 1891 (R72)

'Theatre Royal - Last evening Mr John Levey commenced his second week at the theatre by producing for the first time in Ireland, we are given to understand, a grand new Irish drama entitled Faugh a Ballagh … like those of Garryowen, the scenes of this new play claim a good deal of indulgence from an audience' (*Belfast News Letter*, 13 May 1879).

LONDON, William

ON WEDNESDAY evening between eight and nine o'clock, John Cantillon Heffernan of Manister having occasion to go into his garden, on his return to the house, through the shrubbery, he saw a person lurking in it, and Mr Heffernan called several times to him to stand and tell his business, on which the fellow retreated. Mr H got out of the garden and, joined by a servant boy, whom he left at the hall-door, went down the lawn by the side of the shrubbery, continuing to call to the man therein to surrender himself, which calls of Mr H and his boy on being heard by Mr Furnell and Mr Dwyer who were sitting in the parlour, they ran to Mr H's assistance; when the fellow that was in the shrubbery heard those gentlemen come out, he retreated to the corner of the shrubbery to get over the ditch, but the servant having got thereon and Mr H having advanced into the shrubbery, the man lay concealed and Mr H sent Mr Dwyer in for his guns, while Mr H and Mr F and the servant continued calling out to the man in the shrubbery to surrender and account for himself. When Mr D returned with the guns he gave one to Mr H. On the female servant's return to the kitchen, she told Wm

London (who was groom and confidential servant of Mr H) that his master was attached and the fire arms were gone out, on which London ran out calling on the other servants to follow him to his master's assistance – he, London, having passed to the rere of Mr H along the ditch of the shrubbery, got out of it just at the corner the fellow lay concealed in. Mr H conceiving London to be the lurking fellow from his having come from the corner of the shrubbery, and not being aware of his being out, called to him several times not to run and to give himself up, or that he would fire on him – London continued running towards the ditch to prevent the concealed fellow from getting over, never conceiving that he was the person repeatedly called to, did not reply, and just as he London was going to jump on the ditch, Mr H fired and shot him through the top of the shoulder. On it being ascertained who was shot, Mr H being inconsolable was brought in and the servant remained with London while assistance and light was getting to bring him in, and they heard the lurking fellow escape over the ditch. It is hoped the fellow will be yet discovered, as it is a melancholy thing that the honest faithful London should be shot, through the darkness of the night, in endeavouring to assist his master. A coroner's inquest was yesterday held by Mr James Bennett, John Crips and Villiers Peacocke, Esqs, magistrates, also attended, with several respectable gentlemen; and a verdict returned that the deceased came by his death by a gunshot wound he received in a mistake for the lurking fellow that was about the house of Manister.

Freeman's Journal, 16 September 1823 (R64)

McCARTHY, Dan

DAN McCARTHY, Kilafadamore, Kilgarvan, County Kerry, popularly known as Trust Dick, passed out of this world on Thursday 18th inst. He got his name Trusty Dick from James Stephens and Michael Doheny in consequence of the fidelity with which he held the great trust confided to him. They placed their liberty, and perhaps their lives, in his hands, and they were not mistaken. One of the many incidents which occurred during Dick's intercourse with the '48 men may be interesting. At the time when Stephens and Doheny were on the run, Dick happened to go to Cork on business. Every dead wall in the city was posted with proclamations, giving descriptions of the outlaws and offering large rewards for information as to their whereabouts. Dick coolly pulled off one of those proclamations, folded it up, and put in into his pocket. The morning after his arrival home he went to the hill to look after his cattle, and was surprised to see two strange gentlemen reclining on the heather. He knew them well, but he pretended not. He went towards them and after looking at them closely for a few seconds, pulled out his proclamation, and looked at it and then alternately three or four times. 'Well upon my word', said he, 'you are pretty well described here'. They regarded him with looks of wonder not unmingled with fear, but Dick did not leave them long in suspense. 'Now' said he, 'Come with me and you are safe'. They however were afraid, as they had been seen in the locality the evening before, and having thanked Dick for his offers of hospitality, they hid themselves in the hill till dusk and crossed the country to the opposite side of the parish. They called to the house of a farmer named Twomey and asked for accommodation for the night. Their request having been granted they sent Twomey to the village for groceries etc, giving him a sovereign to pay for them. He purchased the groceries and tendered the sovereign but the grocer told him that he need not mind changing the sovereign that he had time enough to pay. 'Oh, it is not mine at all' said Twomey, 'two strange gentlemen that called to my house that sent me'. Some persons who were present, one of them being the sergeant of police, overheard the remark, but if the sergeant picked any meaning out of it he kept the knowledge strictly to himself. Stephens and Doheny, on hearing what had occurred did not wait for the refreshments but crossed the country again and put themselves in Dick's hands. Dick had an uninhabited house about half a mile from his residence and there he put up the fugitives. He made them as comfortable as he could, brought them their meals regularly every day, and kept the affair so secret that some of the members of his own family did not know it. When they were there about a month their hiding place was found out by an accident. Whenever Dick had occasion to visit them he always signalled his approach by a whistle. One day they heard a whistle and thinking it was Dick, they opened the door and peeped out but what was their amazement when they beheld not their benefactor but a boy who was whistling for his dog. They left the place on that night giving Dick many blessings, which was the only reward he would accept. This is only one of the innumerable services Dick rendered to many of the '48 men, and to relate even a tithe of them would occupy entirely too much space. Not long ago, he was telling a story about Stephens, and when he had finished he took from his pocket a likeness of the Fenian chief and 'there he is, the same age as myself'. For many years the son of prosperity has not shone upon poor Dick. He met many reverses, and worst of it lost his wife about twelve years ago. Since her death he has had a hard struggle with the world, and has left his family in a very embarrassed condition. His friends here have started a fund for the orphans, and when it is remembered how he spurned the thousands that were at one time within his reach, there can be no doubt as to the propriety of the movement. Yes, thousands within his reach, for he had at one time or another most of the principal '48 men in his power, but he was Trusty Dick and remained so to the last.

Kerry Sentinel, 23 March 1897 (R71)

McCARTHY, Florence

WE ARE sure that every one of his old pupils who may glance his eye over this obituary will drop a tear to the memory of Florence McCarthy Esq, AM, late principal of the Killarney Academy. Placed at the head of a seminary still fondly remembered by thousands as the 'College' of Killarney, his scholars consisted of young gentlemen of every religious denomination, and never did a man occupy his responsible position, more faithfully protect the religious principles of each and all, or more sedulously inculcate good feelings and brotherly love among those committed to his charge. Indeed, we believe that it is to the spirit of his teaching that we are to trace much of that absence of religious acrimony which characterises the social intercourse of those gentlemen of both persuasions resident in and about Killarney, who received any portion of their education at his hands. Mr McCarthy sent some able men to Trinity College, which university he had entered himself in the year '98, winning his way to honours, no easy task for a Roman Catholic in those days. Among those men of

marked ability whom he gave to Alms, we may mention
Denis Murphy, known to his contemporaries as a man of
giant intellect, the writer of a powerful paper on the
Catholic Association, and several humorous papers in
Tait's Magazine; Henry O'Brien, author of the learned
work on the Round Towers; John Leahy, of the Munster
Bar, who obtained a scholarship at the early age of
seventeen, and many more who have passed to other
lands or into eternity, and have faded from the memory
of our Kerry readers. For ourselves we will say, with
much humility, but with grateful pride, that if we possess
any ability as a public writer, we owe it to his teaching.
In addition to his classical attainments, our deceased
friend was a distinguished Irish scholar, speaking and
writing the mother tongue with great fluency. Often
have we listened to the old man, as, with a vernacular
energy racy of the soil he loved and gloried in through
life, he recited his own poetic composition in that
language, or his vigorous translations of Homer into the
same old and expressive tongue. But we are no longer
scholars, and must turn away to the rough work of the
world, leaving our early and venerated friend to the long,
long sleep of the grave. Mr McCarthy, on Tuesday last,
passed to 'that bourne whence no traveller returns' in
the 84th year of his age, and on Thursday was borne to
his last home in Muckross Abbey, followed by a large
concourse of friends, including some thirty of the Roman
Catholic clergy of the diocese.

Freeman's Journal, 17 July 1852 (R32)

MacCARTHY, John George (Died 1892)

WE REGRET to have to announce today the death of
Mr John George MacCarthy, the well-known Land
Purchase Commissioner. His disappearance from the
office which he so long held will be a public loss. Few
Irish judges won such public confidence as he had won
by his independence and manifested resolve to
administer the law for the good of the people. Such
successes as the Ashbourne Act had achieved were
due to his efforts. As far as the law gave him power he
resisted all attempts to coerce the people into giving
exorbitant prices for their land. Wherever he saw
evidence of duress he sought it out; and the plan of
using coercion and eviction to force impossible contracts
upon the people met with a stout resistance. Mr
MacCarthy sat once as the Home Rule member for
historic Mallow. His purposes and his character were
good; had he been less hampered by bad laws he would
have left even a better memory.

Edited from *Freeman's Journal*, 8 September 1892 (R77)

McGILLYCUDDY, Anna (Unknown date – 1892) nee Johnstone, daughter of Captain William Johnstone of Maidstone Court, Herefordshire and Miss Hutton

THE ANNOUNCEMENT of the death of Madam MacGillycuddy, widow of Richard 'The MacGillycuddy of the Reeks' appears today. The sad event occurred after two days illness at Aghadoe House, Killarney, the residence of her son, John MacGillycuddy, Esq. The cause of death was influenza. On Thursday the funeral took place. An immense gathering of people attended, even though the weather was most inclement, to testify their affection for the deceased lady. There were representatives of all the county families in attendance. The funeral went from Aghadoe to Knockane Churchyard, where is the family vault. The service was conducted by Rev Joseph Madden, rector and Rev Wm Godfrey. The deceased lady will be much missed in the cottages of the poor in the district, where her generosity was so well known.

Obituary from *The Kerry Evening Post*, 16 January 1892 (R7)

McGILLYCUDDY, Richard (1790-1866) 'of the Reeks', son of Francis McGillycuddy and Catherine Mahony of Dromore

IT IS OUR painful duty this evening to record the death of one of our Kerrymen of mark and the representative of one of the few Irish families which still retain a title to mark their ancient nobility and a fortune equal to their high social position. Richard McGillycuddy, otherwise called The McGillycuddy of the Reeks, died on Saturday, aged 76, at his temporary residence, 6 Upper Pembroke St, Dublin after a protracted and painful illness. He was a Deputy Lieutenant of this county, and possessed considerable property and much influence in Kerry. In his younger days The McGillycuddy was an active magistrate, and, until he gave place to younger men he was one of our most useful grand jurors, and influential fiscal authorities. His politics were Liberal, but not extreme, and his kindness and hospitality gained him deservedly many friends by whom his decease will be regretted. His death was caused by a prolonged attack of bronchitis, but he had suffered much last year from ill health, and it was quite apparent to his friends at that time, hat notwithstanding his recovery the end was near. His remains will be removed on Wednesday for interment in the family vault at Knockane churchyard near Whitefield, Killarney. The McGillycuddy was a generous landlord, a disinterested friend, and thoroughly amiable in all the relations of life. The McGillycuddy was twice married – first to Margaret, only daughter of James Bennett Esq, of Cork by whom he had issue – four sons, who all died unmarried, and three daughters, of whom two died unmarried, and the third became the wife of William Leader Esq, of Rosnalie, who died in 1861, and whose brother Nicholas is now MP for Cork county. The McGillycuddy married secondly, Anna, daughter of Captain William Johnstone, of Maidstone Court, Herefordshire, and by her had issue – ten children, of whom nine survive. Captain Johnstone was in the 3rd Dragoon Guards, in which regiment he served with distinction during the Peninsula War. This is one of the leading branches of the late Marquis of Annadale's family. Her mother, Miss Hutton, was also of a distinguished family, and lineal descendant of the line of Plantagenets. The lady survives The McGillycuddy.

Obituary from *The Kerry Evening Post*, 10 January 1866 (R6)

MAHONY, Daniel (c1794-1871)

DEATH OF Mr Daniel Mahony, JP, Dunloe Castle: This gentleman died at his residence, which takes the name after the far-famed Gap of Dunloe, on Sunday last, in his 77th year. Through life he was of a retiring disposition; simple and unostentatious in his manner, and possessed of a kindly disposition towards his tenantry. He belonged to the oldest of the aristocratic families in the neighbourhood of Killarney. Though having lived to the above good old age, they who have enjoyed his friendship best know how irreparable his loss will be felt in the far-famed regions in which he resided. As a Catholic he was a steadfast one. As a politician he was a strong Conservative. In his character as such, it is within the memory of several in Killarney that, at the great Repeal demonstration held in the old racecourse - the scene of many a social gathering in the good old days – in the year 1844 at which Mr Denis Shine Lawlor presided, and which was attended by Smith O'Brien, Meagher, and a host of the elite of the Repeal

Association, Mr Mahony opposed the adoption of a resolution in honour of the liberation of the great Daniel O'Connell. His acts as a public man – whether as a politician, a magistrate or a poor law guardian – arose mainly from his honesty of purpose, whilst he gratified an honourable ambition, but sought no private or personal desire. His chief consideration was his duty to his conscience. His mourning family and relatives have the consolation that the whole community participate in their grief. His remains were deposited in the old family vault at Aghadoe church, followed by a very large cortege of the elite and others of Killarney and the neighbourhood in which he resided. The deceased's father was Brigade Major in the Kerry Yeomanry.

Kerry Evening Post, 17 May 1871 (R40)

See Froude's account of the Mahonys of Dunloe in *Dunboy: The Murder of John Puxley* at www.lulucom

MAHONY, Harold Segerson (1867-1905)

THERE WILL not be a lawn tennis player in this country
to whom the sad news of H S Mahony's death will not
cause unfeigned regret. To all his intimate friends the
sudden demise of this true, frank, and generous
sportsman occasions the deepest sorrow. The tragedy
is all the more real because it has taken place at the
very height of the All England Championships meeting
at Wimbledon – a carnival at which for the past 20 years
Mahony had not only been a dominant personality but
an active, and on many occasions, a brilliant performer.
His absence from the present gathering – an absence
which had been remarked on by all the old habitués,
was occasioned by the fact that he had gone to Ireland
late in April to attend the sick bed of an ailing uncle, and
for this reason he had not been able to participate in any
of the leading British tournaments this season. Mahony
had won the championship of Middlesex, Berkshire, and

Kent last year, but was prevented from defending these cups. It was fully expected that he would have returned in time for the Wimbledon meeting, and his name appeared in the list of entries. How he would have revelled in the great revival of interest revealed in his favourite game by the colossal entry this year! For no man had a keener or deeper affection for the pastime, or was more anxious for its prosperity. As a player, no bare outline of his numberless achievements can suffice to proclaim his fame, for he was something more than a brilliant prize-winner. From the day that he became Singles Champion of Dublin University in 1889 he never really looked back. The Irish Championship, the English Championship, countless County Championships, trophies abroad, some won on grass, others on sand and on wood floors, and last, but by no means least, his selection to do battle for his country against the Americans in the States – these and many other honours came his way, all being received with a natural modesty yet joyous relish which characterise all true sportsmen. In recent years, although as strenuous and as vigorous as ever in the courts, there had been some slight decline in the accuracy of his game; but just at the moment when people were beginning to think that he had seen his greatest triumphs, a dashing victory and a recrudescence of his matchless talent would be forthcoming. He had many claims to distinction as a player, but it was in volleying especially that his great strength lay. His back-hand smash, the envy of every tyro and a model for even seasoned exponents, won him many an ace outright, and was largely instrumental in making him mixed Doubles Champion of England on five consecutive occasions. Eminently effective too, was his service, always delivered with a grace and deliberation very pleasing to the onlooker. He could place his deliveries with rare judgment, and liked nothing better than to deceive his opponent by varying the direction. 'Make your man move', was his favourite advice to young players learning to serve. His back-hand drive off the ground, too, was another of his pet shots, especially the stroke which skimmed the net from left to right and found the centre line in a double. Mahony may justly be described as an all-round sportsman, for lawn tennis was not the only pastime at which he excelled. He won prizes at swimming, sailing, and pigeon-shooting and could run up his fifty break at billiards without an effort. A the more ancient game of 'real' tennis, to which he also devoted much attention, he was an expert performer, and secured three handicaps at Queen's Club; while as a salmon fisher his zeal and capacity were unquestioned, and many a fine specimen had his rod captured in the wild regions of county Kerry, where he met his tragic death. Apart from all his triumphs on the lawn tennis court – and perhaps no man living has prosecuted the game in public over a longer period or with such a brilliant record – Mahony's personality must survive for many a day. His sunny, genial temperament, his fathomless fund of Irish wit, and smiling eagerness to give advice to young players of both sexes were factors which had endeared his name to a wide circle. While other men grumbled at the failure of their partners, H S Mahony never did; on the contrary, he would be lavish with encouraging remarks, always wearing an unruffled front in the time of adversity. When he ejected good humoured diatribes at the state of the court or weather, these criticisms fell on willing ears, for there was always a spice of wit behind his remarks. For most umpires he had the greatest respect, but there was one occasion when the recurrence of many wrong decisions awoke something like disgust. He gave a sententious look to the official, whereupon the latter asserted that he was not going to be browbeaten, even by the champion of England. 'I was looking at you more in sorrow than in anger' was the instant retort. On another occasion – it was Old Trafford, two seasons back – the Irishman expressed his contempt for ceremony and his disgust for the drenched condition of the turf by removing his shoes and finishing the match in his socks, much to the amusement of the spectators. One recalls too, his trip to Portugal and the evident zest with which he instructed King Carlos, who was his opponent, in the delicate art of mixed double play. When at Homburg, King Edward had more than once witnessed Mahony's play, subsequently conversing with the genial Irishman on the accepted principles of the game. The ex-champion, who was a JP for his native county, will be sorely missed at Queen's Club, which was practically his home while in London; indeed, it would be difficult to name a court in England or abroad where his death, at the early age of thirty-eight, will not evoke expressions of sincere regret.

Obituary published in *The Kerry Evening Post*, 5 July 1905 (R5). A sketch of the Mahonys of Dromore can be found in *Richard John Mahony of Dromore, a Nineteenth Century Gentleman* at www.lulu.com

MAHONY, Richard John (1827-1892)

THE DEATH is reported of Mr Richard J Mahony, D.L.
of Dromore Castle, County Kerry. The head of one of
the oldest county families in Munster, Mr Mahony has
long been a prominent figure in many spheres of activity
in Ireland. As a practical agriculturist he held a very
high place and in the land controversy of recent years
Dromore was constantly referred to as a pattern estate.
Its condition when the Land Act confiscated the results
of his life's work was thus described by the Land
Commissioners who adjudicated upon the fair rent
cases in South Kerry: 'For what is counted a generation
Mr Mahony has applied himself to the improvement of

his estate. He has opened it up by a great series of roads; he has connected it with many bridges; he has made many miles of drains and fences; he has reclaimed hundreds of acres; he has stimulated his tenants' improvements and respected whatever rights were thus created; he has helped his tenants in their troubles with his advice, his capital, and his command of his banking facilities; he has established model farms and model dairies, introduced better breeds of cattle, and by his own admirable example showed his tenants how to improve their stock. His rents rarely exceed the reduced rents which were fixed at the time of the famine'. In a leading article on the Land Act, the *Freeman's Journal*, a notoriously hostile critic of landlords, declared, 'His estate is an oasis in the desert, and has attracted the attention of all travellers and press correspondents to the district'. *The Crime and Penalty of Ownership*, an open letter to Mr Gladstone, is the title of one of several brilliant pamphlets from Mr Mahony's pen calling attention to the mischief and injustice worked by the statute upon estates of such a character. A few articles in *Fraser's Magazine*, contributions obtained from him by Mr J A Froude when in former years he was a frequent visitor to Dromore, also serve to show Mr Mahony's literary abilities. As a speaker Mr Mahony possessed in a marked degree the special graces of Irish oratory without any of its extravagancies, and at the great landlords' meeting of eight years ago, his speech was one of the chief events of the conference. Born at Dromore 65 years ago, he was educated in England and graduated at Oxford University. He died in London last Thursday evening, and was buried on Tuesday in the family vault near Dromore Castle.

Obituary published in *The Kerry Evening Post*, 31 December 1892 (R4). A sketch of the Mahonys of Dromore can be found in *Richard John Mahony of Dromore, a Nineteenth Century Gentleman* at www.lulu.com. A note on Rev Denis Mahony, father of Richard John, who ministered at Templenoe Church of Ireland, is included in the publication, *The Church of Ireland in Co Kerry: a record of church and clergy in the nineteenth century* and is available at www.lulu.com

MURPHY, William Esq

IT HAS seldom fallen to our lot to announce the death of one whose loss will be more deeply deplored. The honourable and intelligent discharge of his public duties, during a long and professional career, and the exercise of the eminent social virtues which adorned his private life, placed Mr Murphy in contact with a large circle of friends both in his native county and in Dublin, who knew how to appreciate his worth whilst living, and who will long feel the blank that his death causes amongst them. Gifted with rare qualities of head and heart, he was remarkable for a sound judgment, a quick appreciation of character, and a knowledge of dealing with men, which, added to large experience and high honour, placed him in the first rank of his profession whilst a noble hospitality and a boundless charity won for him the esteem and love of all classes in his native place, where he lived and died, and where his worth was best known. The loss of such a man must be deeply felt in any society – to his friends and intimates it is irreparable.

Freeman's Journal, 20 November 1860 (R70)

NAGLE, David

THIS DAY, three of the wretched victims to a blind and infatuated policy will atone with their lives for their crimes. The names of the unfortunate men are William McDonnell, David Nagle, and William Noonan, the two former for the attack on the Glebe-house of the Rev Thomas Townsend, at Farrihy, in the open day, and robbing it of arms; and the latter for the attack on the house of George Rogers, Esq, at Knockbarry, near Buttevant.

Morning Post, 12 August 1823 (R66)

'The Dublin papers state that the Captain Rock, in the North Liberties of Cork, and two of his associates, who planned and assisted to execute most of the outrages in that part of the country, have been apprehended by the country people ... The labours of Hercules were so numerous, it is supposed that there were many heroes of that name, and that one of them obtained credit for the labours of all. It is so with Captain Rock. It is now ascertained that the outrages of the South have produced several Captains Rock' (*Morning Post*, 9 July 1823).

'Michael McDonnell, Thomas Sullivan, and David Nagle were indicted for having on the 30th May last, at Farrihy, in this county, attacked the house of the Rev Thomas Townsend, and for having feloniously carried away certain arms, the property of that Gentleman ... John McDonnell was examined for the defence of Nagle, and swore he had been at work for him on the day of the attack from the morning until two o'clock; had been trenching potatoes; he left Nagle for some time in the morning, but when he returned he found him still at work' (*Morning Post*, 26 July 1823).

O'CALLAGHAN, Charles, Staff Surgeon

IT IS LITTLE more than two months since the painful
duty devolved upon us of writing the obituary of Staff
Surgeon Charles O'Callaghan, a native of Killarney, who
died at Cape Coast Castle, West Africa, in the bloom of
manhood, and it was but a few days ago that his
esteemed father, Mr Daniel O'Callaghan, of Killarney,
received a case containing the military uniform and the
various medals presented to the deceased for his
valour. The medals include the Legion of Honour, which
he highly prized. This latter mark of distinction was
conferred by the Emperor of the French only on ten or
twelve of the officers who were engaged at the taking of
the Redan in the memorable Russian war. The case
also contained a most valuable gold watch and chain,
several gold rings, richly ornamented with diamonds and
precious stones, together with other trinkets of intrinsic
worth. Sad as has been the deprivation caused by the
early demise of such an honoured son, it cannot but be
some consolation to his father, in the near and yellow
leaf of life, as well as to the other members of his family,
to have these flattering reminiscences of his bravery and
success, added to the many others which he had left at

home when departing for the fatal sphere of his duties. There was one peculiar incident of his life worthy of notice which did not appear in our obituary. Surgeon O'Callaghan having been a staunch Roman Catholic, and a Mr Gartland, a brother officer, countryman and Catholic, having died in Africa, there was no priest nearer than 600 miles, therefore it was impossible to procure his services. The corpse was borne to the grave on the shoulders of six black soldiers, followed by the colonel, the officers, and men, and accompanied by a Protestant clergyman. On arriving at the cemetery the clergyman insisted that it was his right to read the burial service. Surgeon O'Callaghan came forward and said he would not permit him to do so, inasmuch as the deceased gentleman had bequeathed his body to him and that if its interment was not left to his sole management he would take it away and dispose of it as he pleased. The clergyman then yielded his pretended claims, and Doctor O'Callaghan read the Catholic burial service over his departed friend. These acts were additional laurels in the life and character of Surgeon O'Callaghan, the fighting doctor of the 62nd Regiment of Crimean notoriety, whose name should occupy a prominent position in the list of illustrious Kerrymen, who have made themselves conspicuous for indomitable courage and eminent achievements. As a mark of their appreciation of the qualities of the deceased, Lord and Lady Castlerosse paid a visit to the family to sympathise with them in their affliction, so did the Lord Bishop of Kerry, and many of the leading priests of the diocese.

Freeman's Journal, 4 December 1868 (R30)

O'CONNELL, Morgan (1803-1885)

WE REGRET to announce the death of Mr Morgan
O'Connell, the second son of the Liberator, at the
advanced age of 82 years, the melancholy event having
occurred last evening at the residence of the deceased,
12 Stephen's-green. The gentleman whose death we
record took no part in Irish public life for the last forty
years; indeed, but for the interest naturally felt in the
vicissitudes of the great Tribune's family, it might be
inexcusable to make his demise the subject of notice.
Those who knew him only in the later period of his life
may not have thought it possible that the quiet, dignified,
elderly gentleman of their acquaintance was in his hot
youth a dashing soldier on far foreign fields. And yet it
was the case. Few are now living who remember the
visit of General Devereux to Dublin in the year 1819. He
came on behalf of one of the newly founded Republics
of South America, then struggling for existence against
the enfeebled power of Spain, to enlist what military aid

the Irish could give in the cause of freedom. "The Irish South American Legion" was thus embodied, and one of the officers who purchased a commission in it was Morgan O'Connell. But the enterprise was woefully mismanaged; there was no commissariat organisation on board the ships, and the consequence was that the entire force almost perished on the voyage for want of the necessaries of life. Ultimately they were disembarked on an island in the Spanish main, Santa Margarita, where many died from sheer starvation.

Portion, however, of the expedition, under the leadership of a brother of the famous Fergus O'Connor, effected a junction with Bolivar, the insurgent commander, and to their prowess the final success of the Republican arms was chiefly due. Young O'Connell returned to Ireland after a few years, but only to again seek foreign service in the Austrian army. His wanderings at length over, he settled down at home, but he had no smelt hostile powder for the last time. It was well known that after the fatal termination of his duel with D'Esterre, Daniel O'Connell vowed that he would never again be a party to an encounter of the kind. Whether this knowledge emboldened them or not, it is certain that some of his political opponents sent him challenges which they never desired to be accepted. It happened that in the course of the Session of 1835 O'Connell, carried away by the heat of debate, referred to a certain Lord Alvanley, who had attached him in the Upper House, as 'a bloated buffoon'. Alvanley demanded satisfaction, which Morgan O'Connell offered to give, in lieu of his father. After some hesitation the offer was accepted, and a meeting took place. The author of the Greville Memoirs thus describes the affair, and it is well to remember that he always displays the utmost acrimony in speaking of the O'Connells: 'There was a meeting at De Ros's house, of De Ros, Damer, Lord Worcester, and Duncombe to consider what was to be done on the receipt of Morgan O'Connell's letter, and whether Alvanley should fight him or not ... it was agreed that no time should be lost ... Damer ought not to have consented to the third shots upon any account'. The reference to the third shots is explained by the fact that O'Connell, who was thoroughly in earnest in his fighting, insisted upon carrying on the duel to the bitter end. For this he was denounced as an Irish savage by the English newspapers of the day. At this time he was a Member of Parliament, as he represented Meath from 1834-40, his colleague being a son of the immortal Grattan. In politics however, Morgan O'Connell was never in perfect accord with his great father, and his retirement from Parliament was probably caused by his inability to fall in with the Repeal movement. Thenceforth he dropped completely out of public life, and after some time accepted a place in the office of the Registracy of Deeds. This he held until about fifteen years ago, when he retired owing to age and enfeebled health, and since then he has lived in quiet retirement. During his last illness Mr O'Connell was sedulously attended by Dr Murphy, Harcourt Street, but professional skill was of no avail to avert the fatal termination. In fact, had it not been for the marvellous constitution of the patient, the end would have been sooner.

Freeman's Journal, 21 January 1885 (R55) Lord Alvanley (pictured above) duelled with O'Connell in 1835

O'KEEFFE, Father

IT IS MANY a long day since the town of Killarney witnessed such a spectacle as that seen on Friday last on the occasion of the funeral of Father O'Keeffe, the late parish priest. Father O'Keeffe was a man who well deserved the affectionate esteem and respect of all classes and all creeds. He was born forty-six years ago near Cuillan, in the county of Cork. In his boyhood there lingered on still in the various towns of the diocese of Kerry those classical schools which won for Kerry in the last century the reputation of being the most learned county in Ireland. It was at one of these that Father O'Keeffe received his early education. After being well grounded in the two great languages of Greece and Rome, Father O'Keeffe entered Maynooth. It was in the native language of his country however, that he distinguished himself most. He was ordained in Maynooth 1870. In his missionary career his sermons in Irish were regarded as models of vigorous, dignified, simple pulpit oratory. He was sent as curate from Tralee to Killarney by the late Dean Mawe. In 1889 he was appointed parish priest of Killarney. In the many important subjects claiming his attention as the spiritual guide of a large flock there was one to which he specially devoted his attention – the organisation and maintenance of confraternities. In instruction of children and the visitation of his schools Father O'Keeffe never spared himself. Though never of a robust constitution his health on the whole was fairly good until a short time before his last attack of illness. In a drive to Glengariffe in an open car he met with a slight accident, and was detained in the open air under a heavy shower for several hours. This led to a chill, and a severe cold, which settled on the lungs. After a few weeks he rallied, but the improvement was only temporary, and he removed to Boherbue Presbytery, the residence of his uncle, the Rev Cornelius Sheahan. He was perfectly resigned and passed peacefully away on September 10th at 4pm. The remains were brought to the Cathedral, Killarney on the following day, and the funeral took place on Friday. His cousin, the Rev Patrick Lynch, M.R., sang the Mass. Two other cousins, the Rev Denis Sheahan, Salford, and the Rev Peter Sheahan, were deacon and sub-deacon. The funeral cortege started for the old cemetery at Kilcummin, where members of Father O'Keeffe's family have been buried for generations. At the head of the procession was the Most Rev Dr Coffey. Then came more than half the priests of the Diocese of Kerry, 62 in number, many of them from a distance and at great personal inconvenience. The clergy marched in procession in cassock and surplice before the hearse. Immediately after were the chief mourners – the Rev Cornelius Sheahan, uncle; Rev Fathers James Sheahan,

Bartholomew Scanlan, Cornelius Kiely, Patrick Lynch, Denis Sheahan, Timothy Crowly, Peter Sheahan, and Charles McCarthy, all cousins of the deceased; his brother, Mr B O'Keeffe, and his sisters, Mrs O'Leary, Mrs Hickey, Mrs O'Donoghue, Mrs Dennehy, and Mrs Buckley. The children of Mary and the children of the two convent schools and the monastery school walked in procession, wearing black crape bands on the arm. The general public followed, and the enormous number may be imagined when it is stated that the funeral was a mile and three quarters in length. Lord Kenmare was present at the funeral, and stood at the grave as the Bishop read the funeral service. The coffin was covered with a multitude of floral wreaths. They were sent by all classes of the community. Lord and Lady Kenmare, Lady Castlerosse and Lady Margaret Douglas sent each a wreath. Wreaths were also sent by the Sisters of the Presentation and Mercy Convents, Loretto Covent, the Women's Confraternity of the Holy Family, Mr and Mrs McDonagh, Mrs Loughlan, Mrs Brooks, Miss Coffey, Mrs Murphy, Mr and Mrs Courtnay, Miss McCarty, Mr and Mrs T O'Conner, Mrs Leonard, and from many more. Amongst the clergy who attended were the Rev Fathers Hayes, Byrne, Fuller and Murphy (curates at the Cathedral), O'Leary, President Brennan, Dowling, O'Flaherty, Scanlan (professors St Brendan's Seminary), O'Leary, Senior Dean Maynooth; T O'Donoghue, Cloyne; L Fuller, PP Kilcummin.

Freeman's Journal, 17 September 1895 (R29)

O'REARDON, Dr (1776-1866)

DR O'REARDON, whose death took place on Wednesday last at Killarney had reached the patriarchal age of ninety and was the oldest member of the College of Physicians. Under the patronage of his uncle, the late Most Rev Dr Sugrue, Bishop of Kerry, Mr O'Reardon entered in 1797 the College of Maynooth where he received instruction from Dr De La Hogue and the Rev John Chetwode Eustace, author of the' Classical Tour of Italy'. A pause in his speech having unfitted him for the pulpit, he relinquished theological for physiological studies and in 1802 he became a physician. During this year he published in Latin some medical dissertations, dedicated to Doctors Clarke and Purcell. Sound sense, free from the theorising flights to which some young physicians are prone, characterise these productions while their Latinity is pure and vigorous. In 1803 Dr O'Reardon proceeded to France for the purpose of gathering experience at the hospitals of that city and of enjoying the advantages of a course of botanical instruction under the celebrated Baron Cuvier. Prolonged hostilities between France and England sprung up shortly after and Dr O'Reardon, together with his grand uncle, the General Count O'Connell, of the British service, with whom he resided, were detained in

France until the restoration of the Bourbons, nine years later. The longevity of the family is remarkable, General O'Connell having attained the age of 91 at his death in 1834. In 1814, Dr O'Reardon returned to Ireland and became physician to some public institutions, from which he received formal addresses of thanks; but it is in connection with the fever hospital in Cork-street with which he will be chiefly remembered. For thirty years he was, with the late Dr Harkin, its zealous and efficient medical attendant; but on the reduction of the hospital grants in 1848 his services were relinquished. The medical reports of the hospital, of which many exist, from his pen, attest the unremitting zeal with which Dr O'Reardon watched over the patients committed to his care. He was also the writer of a small memoir of Kirwan, the eminent chemist, whose friendship he possessed. He was the associate in consultation with Colles, Chayne, Crampton, and Carmichael; and although he did not hold quite as high a rank as those eminent names, he largely shared their friendship and high opinion. Dr O'Reardon was first-cousin of the illustrious Daniel O'Connell, whose family physician he had been. The infirmities of age led to his retirement from the profession, and a few years ago he removed to Mount Prospect, overlooking the Lakes of Killarney, where he tranquilly breathed his last, almost on the spot where he was born. He had been always remarkable for practical piety; and it may with truth be said that the whole tenor of his long life was one uninterrupted preparation for the next.

Freeman's Journal, 17 March 1866 (R38)

O'SULLIVAN, Theodore (1705-1820)

IN THE parish of Aglish, in the vicinity of Killarney, at the very advanced age of one hundred and fifteen years, Theodore O Sullivan, the celebrated Irish bard. This extraordinary man, who was a great composer in his native language, expired suddenly on Wednesday last, whilst sowing oats in the field of one of his great grandchildren, and retaining his faculties to the last moment! He is said to have sung to the plough one of his favourite lyrics and actually breathed his last at the final stanza of his national melody. The deceased also followed the occupation of a cooper, and is said to have made a churn, from which butter was taken for the christening of his twenty-sixth great grandchild.

Freeman's Journal, 6 March 1820 (R51)

POWEL, John (or Powell)

'AT SANDVILLE, Castleisland on 8th inst in the 82 (or 62?) year of his age, Mr John Powel, after a protracted illness. Mr Powel's father was the first English agriculturist that ever came to Kerry and was strongly recommended by the then Earl of Powis in the year 1782 to the great grandfather of the present proprietor of Muckross, Cpt Herbert, MP. Mr Powel found the present beautiful and delightful Muckross a barren waste – unadorned and unimproved, a cover for goats which roamed in myriads, the undisputed occupants of the wild, wide waste. Under Mr Powel's management the fine old oaks and elms of Muckross and the attractive plantations of Torc were planted and matured. As a mark of the faithful services of Mr Powel, the old colonel gave the valuable farm of Sandville, which the Powel family improved and embellished in a husband-like manner. Mr Powel was one of the leading farmers connected with our defunct agricultural shows. He excelled in sheep, and was equal to the best farmer in Kerry in cattle and turnips. There are at this moment on the farm of the deceased the two first iron ploughs that ever came into Kerry. Deceased was always regarded as one of the best judges of land in Kerry and regarded as such by being put on the Tythe Commission. It was deceased also who executed all the planting on the Headley estate, including that of Aghadoe and Rossbeigh.'

Tralee Chronicle and Killarney Evening Echo, 12 March 1867 (R46) 'Died at Sandville, John Frederick, eldest son of James F Powell, in 5th year' (*Kerry Evening Post*, 9 April 1879)

QUILL, Albert William (c1844-1908)

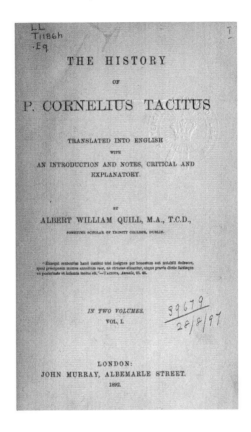

MR ALBERT William Quill, a well-known member of the
Irish Bar, died in Dublin on Saturday in his 64th year. Mr
Quill, who was a native of the county Kerry, was
educated at Trinity College, Dublin. He was a Roman
Catholic, and was one of the few members of that faith
to win a non-foundation classical scholarship in Trinity
College before the abolition of the tests under Fawcett's
Act. Mr Quill was an excellent classical scholar, and his

translation of the History of Tacitus which was issued in two volumes in 1892, was distinguished by much felicity of taste and expression. He was an authority on several branches of law, and was the author of some important works on the Irish Land Acts. One of these, 'The Landowners' and Agents' Practical Guide', has reached an eighth edition. In his more active years, Mr Quill took a keen interest in politics, and was a popular and effective speaker on Irish Unionist platforms.

The Times, 8 February 1908 (R48)

Note: Son of Thomas Quill, bank manager of National Bank Tralee, Wexford, perhaps Waterford and Kingstown. Married in 1874 to Margaret Chute, daughter of Rev James Chute. 'The death has taken place in Kingstown of Mr Thomas Quill, the oldest officer in the employ of the National Bank (Limited). Mr Quill, who was 92 years of age, and had served the bank for 60 years, was appointed to his first post in the bank by its famous founder, Daniel O'Connell' (*Northeastern Gazette*, 28 January 1899).

ROVING Bard (Larry Cotter)

AT THE assizes for the county of Cork, a case came on
to be tried, in which the question to be determined was,
the validity of a will made by his father-in-law, in favour
of a man named John Fitzgibbon. The other relations
contended that the will was spurious, as the deceased
had never been reconciled to his daughter after she was
married. To prove the contrary one Cotter was called,
who is well known under the denomination of The
Roving Bard. This fellow's office is that of Poet Laureate
to the whole county, having no occupation but visiting
the different farmers' houses, and paying for his board
by songs and poems in praise of the hostess and her
family, which are preserved by them as so many records
of their hospitality. The Bard swore that he saw the
deceased at the house of his son-in-law perfectly
reconciled before his death, upon which occasion he
made some very famous verses. Being asked what
these verses were, he rummaged a large bundle of
papers, from which he selected the following sublime
effusion of his gratulatory muse:

Hail, happy union,
John Fitzgibbon!
You and the father of your wife
Will now be friends the remainder of your life.
When Charon takes him into his old boat,
Though grief, alas! Will choak your honest throat,
Yet I shall see you in a bran-new coat.
Your wife and children will be better dressed,
When death leaves you the key of his strong chest.
May your kind love and friendship never totter!
So sings the Roving Bard, sweet Larry Cotter.

When the recitation was over, the Poet looked round to
enjoy those praises he was so much accustomed to,
and beheld the whole Court convulsed with laughter.
This testimony, however, had its full effect; for it
obtained credit with the jury, and established the validity
of the will.

Jackson's Oxford Journal, 22 August 1901 (R67)

SANDES, Elise (1851-1934)

MISS ELISE Sandes, the originator of the Sandes
Soldiers' Homes, which are known in many parts of the
world, died yesterday at Dundrum, Co Down, at the age
of 83. She had been ailing for some time, but
maintained her interest in the work t the last, and she
died in the home attached to Ballykinlar Camp. The
daughter of Mr Stephen Sandes, of Sallow Glen, Co
Kerry, she had a soldier brother, and 66 years ago was
asked to look after the welfare of a little drummer boy in
his regiment. The work grew from that small beginning.
Homes were opened first in Ireland, but they have since
extended to England and Scotland, to India and to
Jamaica. Always she sought to establish the homes in
the remote Army stations where the soldiers in their
leisure would be unable to obtain the comforts which
she provided. Miss Sandes sought always to further the

spiritual welfare of the men, but the religious exercises were entirely optional and un-denominational. The homes were open to all. The Duke of Connaught, Lord Wolseley, and Lord Roberts were all among her personal friends and aided her in her efforts to extend the work. She collected thousands of pounds to carry it on, and did an incalculable amount of good among the men. During the War the homes, which now number 33, were exceptionally busy. Some years ago Miss Sandes published a book explaining the scope of the work under the title "Enlisted" and she edited a monthly paper for soldiers entitled *Forward*. She was made a CBE in 1920. One of the homes was opened at Catterick Camp in November 1928 to celebrate the diamond jubilee of the work.

The Times, 20 August 1934 (R49)

SAUNDERS, Arthur Lloyd (c1811-1847)

DEATH OF Arthur Lloyd Saunders Esq – The Cork and Kerry journals announce the death of this lamented gentleman in his 36th year, at his residence, Flesk Cottage, Killarney. He died on Saturday last of a malignant fever contracted in the discharge of his duties as secretary to the Killarney Relief Committee. Only a few days intervened between the grave and the scene of his most active and unrivalled exertions! Mr Saunders was a remarkable man. Educated in the University of Gottingen, where he had privately studied under the distinguished German writers – Hoeren and Dahlman, his erudition was alike extensive and accurate. The literature and public law of Europe he thoroughly understood. His knowledge of language was also surprising. He spoke with the greatest fluency, French, Italian, German, Spanish, Portuguese and Dutch. Mr Saunders was called both to the English and Irish bars though never in practice. The inheritance of an ample fortune withdrew him from the bar to cultivate the more congenial life of a resident landlord and country gentleman, in both of which characters he was distinguished by the display of virtues such as few men have ever realised. His active mind was incessantly devoted to measures of practical improvement. He loved his country and his fellow countrymen. He thought of nothing but their happiness. Mr Saunders was in politics a Whig. He was not a public character for his gentle nature was averse to the boisterousness of public display. His virtues and affections were all for the circle of his friends in which he was as delightful as he was admired and respected. His manner had all the grace and sweetness of the female sex so that those who did not know him found it difficult to reconcile his amiable and playful deportment with the moral intrepidity which he was known to possess. One of the best managed relief committees in Ireland is the Killarney committee. Its perfect organization and admirable efficiency were owing to Mr Saunders. He worked it without a day's intermission and between thirty and forty thousand mouths were regularly fed. He brought supplies from London, Hamburg, and America and presided at their distribution both by day and by night. The munificence of his private charity and the extent of his public services render his death a national loss. He fell a victim to his chivalrous sense of duty. It is the memory of such men should be cherished who, sacrificing health and repose to the cause of humanity, sink exhausted at their posts like heroic and faithful sentinels.

Edited from *Freeman's Journal*, 5 March 1847 (R36) 'As a grand juror and a magistrate, he was ever found acting up to the strictest principles of honour, and his services in the former capacity in getting rid of turnpikes in Kerry conferred a lasting benefit on those parts of the county affected thereby' (*Kerry Evening Post*, 3 March 1847).

SCOTT, Sir Walter (1771-1832)

SIR WALTER Scott left Killarney this afternoon for Cork.
Previous to his departure he paid a visit to Mr Hallam,
the celebrated author of the *Middle Ages*, who is
confined to his bed in consequence of having broken his
thigh, in a fall from one of the rocks which project from
the Island of Innisfallen over the lake.

Morning Post, 16 August 1829 (R56)

From the few words that Sir Walter Scott uttered, it
could be easily perceived that he has a strong Scotch
accent. Age has blanched his locks, his face is precisely
that which is termed a Scotch face, large and full, with a
prominent nose, good forehead, and a light blue eye. In
fact, he reminded us very much of that worthy man, 'rest

and bless him' Old Mortality .... In the course of the evening there was a cheer for Thomas Moore, whose parents sat in the next box to Sir Walter (extracted from a report of Sir Walter Scott's visit to Dublin, which included a visit to a production of Clari; *Morning Chronicle*, 23 July 1825). Wednesday the honoured remains of Sir Walter Scott were consigned to the tomb ... the streets of Melrose were lined on both sides with the inhabitants in mourning and uncovered. The shops of this and other towns were shut; the sign boards were covered with black; the aged and the lame came forth to pay their last tribute to departed worth; and along the many miles of picturesque country which the procession had to traverse, the ensigns of sorrow were every where displayed ... at Dryburgh Abbey the body, on being taken from the hearse, was borne by his own domestics to the grave, they having specially requested that no foreign hand should be allowed to touch the remains of a master so honoured and so beloved ... sixty-two carriages, phaetons, and gigs followed the hearse – the black plumes of the latter and the cloaks of the mutes on horseback leading the procession ... before the body was committed to the earth, the English Burial Service was read by Rev J Williams, rector of the Edinburgh Academy ... we could not help thinking of his own beautiful words – 'They sleep with him, who sleeps below'.... We understand that Sir Walter's head was opened on Sunday. The left side of the brain was found in a soft state, and there were globules of water under the left lobe, appearances which fully accounted for all the fatal symptoms by which he has been afflicted (*The Scotsman,* 29 September 1832).

SPRING-RICE, Thomas (1st Lord Monteagle)

LORD MONTEAGLE died on Tuesday at Mount Trenchard, his seat in the county Limerick. The late Right Hon Thomas Spring-Rice, Baron Monteagle, of Brandon, county Kerry, in the peerage of the United Kingdom, was the eldest son of the late Mr Stephen Edward Rice, of Mount Trenchard, by Catherine, daughter and heir of Mr Thomas Spring, of Ballycrispin, in the county Kerry. He was born February 8, 1790, and married first, July 11 1811, Lady Theodosia Pery, second daughter of Edward Henry, first Earl of Limerick, which lady died December 10 1839; and he wedded, secondly, April 13 1841, Mary Anne, eldest daughter of the late Mr John Marshall, of Hallsteads, Cumberland. By his first marriage he had a family of nine sons and daughters, his eldest son, who would have succeeded to the title, the Hon Stephen E Spring-Rice, having died in the spring of last year....The eldest son of the late Hon Stephen Edmund Spring-Rice and grandson of the late Lord – namely, Thomas Spring-Rice, born 31st May 1849 – succeeds to the peerage.

The Examiner, 10 Feb 1866 (R63). Image courtesy of the
National Portrait Gallery, www.npg.org.uk.

The funeral of the late Lord Monteagle took place today
from his residence at Mountrenchard, near Foynes. The
weather was exceedingly uninviting, a heavy fall of snow
having been experienced during the morning, which had
the effect of preventing many from distant places
attending; the assemblage was however exceedingly
large, embracing the nobility and gentry of the county,
as well as the farming and labouring classes, who
mustered in strong force upon foot and horseback.
Twelve o'clock was the hour appointed, at which period
the train from Limerick arrived, conveying the Right Hon
the Earl of Dunraven, the Hon Robert O'Brien, Sir
Richard Griffith, Major Vandeleur, William Carroll
(Chamber of Commerce), Sir William Hartigan
Barrington, John Vanderkiste, John Long, CE, John
Barrington (solicitor), Joseph Harvey, CaptainHowley,
Thompson Russel, Michael Robert Ryan, John Ellard,
Dr Worrall (Adare), Thomas Fosberry Esqs, &c. When
the coffin was removed from the grand hall of the noble
mansion it was placed in the hearse, and the procession
moved to Shanagolden Churchyard, a distance of four
miles, in the following order, all the preliminary
arrangements for the extensive cavalcade having been
carried out by Mr Shannon for the undertaker (Mr
Owens) in a most creditable and satisfactory manner.
The female domestics, shrouded in white linen; the
hearses carrying the body; four mourning coaches – the
chief mourners being the three sons of deceased; his
brother-in-law, the Messrs Marshall, the Earl of
Dunraven, the youthful successor of the title; Sir Richard

Griffith, Sir Wm H Barrington, George Fosberry, Sir Vere de Vere, Stephen de Vere, Sir Aubrey de Vere, Hon Edward Pery, Hon Edward O'Brien. A long line of private equipages of the nobility and gentry; two-hundred men on horseback brought up the rere, and over 700 of the tenantry of the families on the property of the late nobleman, the Earl of Dunraven, and the De Veres, marched in front wearing white hat bands. It was computed the cavalcade extended two miles along the road, and when the funeral reached the burying ground the coffin was taken to the interior of the church, where service was read by the Rector of Foynes, assisted by the Rev Joseph Gabbitt, after which the remains were deposited in the family vault. On the lid of the coffin was inscribed – The Right Hon Thomas Spring Rice, first Lord Monteagle of Brandon, born 8 February 1790; died 7th February 1866' (*Freeman's Journal*, 15 Feb 1866).

'The will of the late Right Hon Thos Spring Rice, Baron Monteagle, was proved in London on the 18th ult by his relict, the Right Hon Mary Ann, Baroness Monteagle; his son, the Hon William Cecil Spring Rice; and his nephew, Mr Stephen Edward De Vere of Monana,e Limerick .... All his estate and lands in Castlemaine, Kerry, his mansion at Mount Trenchard, Limerick, and all other his freeholds, devolve to his grandson, Thomas Spring Rice, now in his 17th year' (*Jackson's Oxford Journal*, 16 June 1866). 'The death of the Right Hon S E Spring Rice, eldest son of Lord Monteagle, which took place at sea, on Thursday, while on a cruise for the benefit of his health' (*Nenagh Guardian*, 17 May 1865).

SULLIVAN, T D (c1827-1914)

IT IS WITH deep regret that we have to announce the death of Mr T D Sullivan, ex-MP, the veteran Irish patriot, poet, and journalist, which occurred yesterday morning at his residence in Dublin, in his 87th year. One of nature's gentlemen and Ireland's most gifted sons, 'TD' as he was affectionately called, was one of the foremost of that galaxy of brilliant Irishmen who made 'The Nation' a power in the land. His famous ballad, 'God Save Ireland', was at once regarded as the National Anthem. He was Lord Mayor of Dublin in 1886 and 1887. He suffered imprisonment for two months in Tullamore Jail in 1888 under the Coercion Act for publishing reports of 'suppressed branches' of the Land League. He represented Westmeath in Parliament 1880-85; Dublin City 1885-1892 and West Donegal 1892-1900. He gave evidence before the Parnell

Commission in 1889. He maintained up to the last a lively interest in the struggle for Irish freedom, to which he had devoted his life. Since retiring from his Parliamentary duties, Mr Sullivan spent an uneventful life in the quietness of his family circle. While his health permitted, he frequently visited the old 'Nation' offices. T D Sullivan was born in the town of Bantry. He was the eldest of four brothers, the others being A M Sullivan, D B Sullivan, and Donal Sullivan, all of whom displayed in life the conspicuous ability which came to them as a family inheritance. In July 1818 William Smith O'Brien visited Bantry. The elder Sullivan lost his situation by reason of his connection with the '48 Movement, but he had already secured for his sons the best mental training. It was possible for them to secure in their native town. In later life, TD married his teacher's daughter, Miss Catherine Healy and she proved herself an affection helpmate to her husband amid all the stress of an arduous life. Her death in 1899 was mourned as a serious loss to Dublin charity and philanthropy. It was early in the fifties that A M Sullivan came to Dublin to embark on that active public career which has left such an impress on the political history of the thirty odd years which followed. About the beginning of the same period, TD Sullivan contributed his poems to the 'Nation' which thrilled the hearts of thousands of Irish youths by the virility and true National ring of its writings. It was through his genial gift of poesy that he had accomplished some of his best work for Ireland and established his best claim to permanent remembrance. As a song writer he revealed the possession of a true poetic feeling. His 'Song from the Backwoods' became immensely popular in America in a short time. *Dunboy and Other Poems* was published in Dublin in 1861 and *Green Leaves* appeared previous to the Land League agitation. In 1887 appeared another volume of *Lays of the Land League* and he subsequently brought out *Prison Poems and Lays of Tullamore*. In the same year he published another volume of miscellaneous poems and ballads, and in 1891, *Blanaid and Other Poems*. He was also concerned with 'Irish Penny Readings', 'Emerald Gems', and a collected volume of 'Speeches and Addresses' of the late A M Sullivan. He also wrote a short biography of his brother and other volumes were *A Record of Traitorism, or the Political Life and Adventures of Judge Keogh*; *A Short History of England* and *A Guide to Dublin*. The late Mr Sullivan was the lineal descendant of O'Sullivan Beare.

Edited from *Irish Independent*, 1 April 1914 (R76). O'Sullivan references in Froude's *Dunboy: The Murder of John Puxley* at www.lulu.com

TALBOT, Andrew (1809-1870) Son of James Talbot of
Glanbegh and husband of Harriett Cambridge

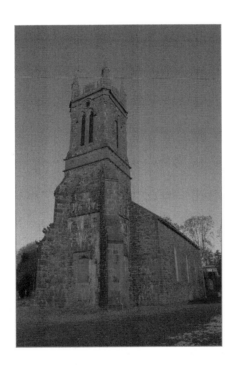

IT IS WITH the sincerest regret I communicate the death
on Wednesday last, at Castleisland, of Andrew Talbot
Esq, Agent to Lord Headley. This afflicting event
occurred whilst the deceased gentleman had been
engaged in collecting rents in the portion of the Headley
estate situate at Castleisland, when he was suddenly
attacked with apoplexy, and immediately after expired.
Anyone who had even the slightest acquaintance with
the deceased would have been prepossessed by the
becoming good nature, kindness, and courtesy of his

demeanour; his disposition fully corresponded with his affable manner. Indeed, few men from the sterling uprightness of principle as well as purity of mind, which characterised him through life, was more esteemed in his public and private capacity and dealings, than Mr Talbot. For in him there was mingled the very type of everything kind, generous and good. For the last twenty-two years, up to the period of his lamented demise, he had acted as agent to the Headley estate in this county, and during that long and trying period he, by his conduct as such, never performed a harsh or inconsiderable act. On the contrary, he was esteemed and loved by the tenantry, as he invariably sought not alone to make them easy and comfortable in their circumstances, but to make them independent of others. Few in his capacity as agent could be found who conciliated their kind regards as well as of the rest of the community. Many an act of kindness is today recorded of him by the tenantry, whilst the management of the estate ever gave equal satisfaction to Lord Headley and his distinguished predecessors. The suddenness of his demise has naturally cast a sad and deep gloom over the inhabitants of Killarney of all grades, classes and creeds; and deep and lasting is, and will be, the regret of the tenantry on the Headley estate. Deceased leaves a widow as beloved as himself, and a young and lovely family to mourn for his untimely loss.

From *The Kerry Evening Post*, 5 March 1870 (R27)

TALBOT-CROSBIE, William (1817-1899)

THE DEATH of William Talbot Crosbie took place on
Monday at his seat, Ardfert Abbey. Mr Talbot-Crosbie
had reached the good old age of 82 years, and was one
of those men to whom Kerry owes much. Ever anxious
for the improvement of his native county, he took an
active interest in his estate, and was one of those who
many years ago inaugurated Kerry Agricultural shows,
our improved cattle owing much to his Ardfert herd. In
early life Mr Talbot-Crosbie was interested in politics,
actively advocating the passing of the Reform Bill. For
many years he has resided quietly at Ardfert, where,
during the last few months, his increasing feebleness
has been an anxiety to his friends. With him has passed

away the last link with the old Corporation of Tralee, William Talbot Crosbie being the last name signed to the Burgess list in March, 1840, the year in which Town Commissioners were appointed – which form of Government was superseded this year by Urban Councillors. Mr Talbot-Crosbie, whose original surname was Talbot, was descended from the sister of the last Earl of Glandore, and when he succeeded to the estates he by patent added the family name of the extinct peerage – Crosbie. The estate included Ardfert Abbey, which, if anything, is a more imposing structure than the celebrated Muckross Abbey, and the ruins of the cathedral, with its magnificent lancet window which has given the name to the present Diocese of Ardfert and Aghadoe. Deceased gentleman was a DL for Kerry, but very many years ago, from religious convictions, he retired from party and politics and also resigned the JP and DL honours, and devoted himself to promote the well-being of his fellow men. He is best known in connection with his celebrated Ardfert shorthorn herd. He commenced its formation as far back as 1846 but it was not until six years after that he commenced the annual sale of young bulls and heifers which has gone on uninterruptedly ever since, increasing in importance each year, and sending representative young sires to every quarter of the globe. He has been the means of doing incalculable good, especially in North Kerry. Mr Talbot-Crosbie, many years ago, ceased to be a member of the then Established church, and joined what are known as the Plymouth Brethren, who recognise no particular sect or creed, and base their faith on the words of the Holy Writ, and if ever there was a true Christian the deceased gentleman was one. After a long illness he passed away full of peace and happiness. It was about a week before the sad event occurred that he said to his medical attendant, Dr Hargrave, 'Doctor, I am sure you are only performing your duty in keeping me alive, but I would rather to be allowed to pass away to my rest and my Redeemer'. The remains, in a suite of coffins, which were covered with beautiful wreaths of white flowers, were laid in the Hall of Ardfert House, which faces and is within a hundred yards of the grand old Abbey. The funeral cortege wended its way through the demesne to the Cathedral ruins, the tenantry to the number of sixty walking in front, and wearing white scarfs and hat bands, and the relatives and friends in large numbers following after. He is succeeded by his eldest son, Leiutenant-Colonel Crosbie, late of the 69th Rifles.

Obituary from *The Kerry Evening Post*, 6th & 9th September 1899 (R16)

TALLON, Elizabeth

WE REGRET to announce the death of Mrs Elizabeth
Tallon of the Royal Victoria Hotel, Killarney which took
place on Friday evening at the advanced age of 76
years. The deceased lady was sister of the late Mrs
Maria O'Leary, of the Royal Victoria Hotel. Her death
has caused deep and universal regret to Killarney and
district, her many excellent qualities endeared her to all
classes of the community, and especially to the poor, by
whom her loss will be keenly felt. The remains were
conveyed to the Cathedral, and at 2 o'clock on Sunday
the funeral started for the New Cemetery, where the
interment took place. The cortege was an extremely
large and representative one, and testified in a marked
degree to the esteem and regard in which the deceased
lady was held. The chief mourners were: J Maher-
Loughnan, JP, CUDC, Dr g Maher-Loughnan, J A J
Brooks, solr, and CPS, Killarney (grand nephews). The
clergy present were His Lordship Most Rev Dr Mangan,
Very Rev M Fuller Adm, VF, Rev J O'Sullivan, PP,
Fossa, Rev D O'Connor, CC, Killarney, Rev D Murphy,

CC, Rev J J O'Connor, CC, Rev P Marshall, VP, St Brendan's Seminary, Rev C J Fitzgerald, BDBCL, do; Rev P O'Carroll, Professor, do. Amongst those who sent wreaths were 'In loving memory from Ethel, John, Bertie and Dudley'; 'In loving memory from May, Daisy, Kathleen, and Harold'; 'In loving memory from Minnie and Jack'; 'In loving memory from Minnie and Tom'; 'With sincere sympathy from the staff Royal Victoria Hotel'.

Kerry Evening Post, 27 January 1909 (R69)

TRENCH, John Townsend (1834-1909) Son of Richard
(William Stueart) Trench married firstly Agnes Merivale
and secondly, in 1874, Leonora Gore Wray of Co
Donegal with whom he had five children

WE REGRET to announce the death of Mr John
Townsend Trench, JP, who was for many years agent
over the Marquis of Lansdowne's estates in the Co
Kerry and who became famous in book and story while
holding that important position. On the public boards in
Kerry in former days Mr Trench was a very prominent
figure and his ability and judgment proved of much
service to his colleagues. He served regularly on the

Grand Jury for this county up to the Spring Assizes of 1898, in which year he fiscal business was transferred to the County Council. About this time he invented the Trench Tubeless Tyre for bicycles and a company was formed to work the patent, but it proved a big failure financially. In the meantime Mr Trench also invented a patent medicine called 'Trench's Remedy' and retired from the Lansdowne agency and went to reside in Dublin, and from thence went to London, and his name has been more or less forgotten in this county. In former years the late Mr Trench was an ardent revivalist, and occupied the pulpit in the Methodist Church in Tralee on more than one occasion. His death took place at Camberley, London on Monday last, in his 75th year, and he was buried at Brompton Cemetery on Thursday.

Obituary from *The Kerry Evening Post*, 14 August 1909 (R8)
Note: An article, 'John Townsend Trench: Land Agent and Preacher', appeared in the 2012 edition of *Bulletin of the Methodist Historical Society of Ireland*, edited by Robin P Roddie, Vol 17 (Number 33) pp39-54.

UNWIN, Thomas Fisher

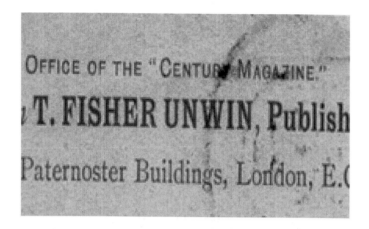

'MR THOMAS Fisher Unwin, a son-in-law of Richard
Cobden, the famous economist, died at his home in
Hayshott, Midhurst, Sussex, aged 87. Mr Unwin was the
founder, in 1882, of the publishing house of Fisher
Unwin. Mrs Fisher Unwin, who survives him, is
Cobden's third daughter'.

Irish Press, 7 February 1935 (R65)

Fisher Unwin published a number of Irish titles, including
the work of George Bartram, whose book, *The White
Headed Boy*, published in 1898, recounted the murder
of John O'Connell Curtin in Kerry. Biographical
information on George Bartram is sought by The
Obituary Book and would be much appreciated.

VENTRY, Lord: Thomas Townsend Aremberg De
Moleyns (Mullins) (1786-1868)

THE FUNERAL of Lord Ventry. Half-past twelve o'clock
on Friday having been fixed for the interment of the
remains of this respected nobleman, long before that
hour, notwithstanding the severity of the day, the
numerous tenantry on the family estates, from far and
near, began to assemble on the lawn at Burnham.
Distinguished as they were by white scarves and hat
bands, they formed in their hundreds an imposing
spectacle. As the hour for the funeral drew near, crowds

of all ranks from Dingle and the surrounding districts were present and the gentry and clergy of all persuasions, not alone from the barony of Corkaguiney, but from Tralee and other more remote parts of the county, had arrived. At a few minutes to one o'clock, the coffin – a handsome polished oak one enclosing the usual lead shell – was borne from Burnham hall-door on the shoulders of his lordship's tenantry. His lordship's four sons, Lord Ventry [Dayrolles], the Hons Frederick, Edward, and Denis De Moleyns, his sons-in-law, Capt Hawkey, RN, Rev Henry J Tomb, and Mr Saunderson, MP, and his grandson, Master Aremberg Chute, and other relatives, walked after the coffin as chief mourners. The burial-place is an old graveyard called Rahenyhuig [*Raithin Ui Bhuaig*], just outside the demesne wall, and in which several members of the De Moleyns family had been previously interred. The procession, which was composed of some 4,000 people, moved on through the grounds, out of the avenue gate, and along a road running round the demesne, and on by the verge of the Dingle harbour for nearly two miles to the graveyard, where the Rev John Chute, his lordship's chaplain, performed the burial service, after which the remains of the late Lord Ventry were committed to the tomb amid every mark of respect that could be paid to his memory by his family, his friends, his tenantry, and his neighbours.

Belfast News Letter, 28 January 1868 (R47) Note: Image depicts Lord Ventry's son, Dayrolles (1829-1914), 4th Baron Ventry

WHITTY, Michael James (c1795-1873)

PRESENTATION TO Mr M J Whitty: A gathering of a
character rarely precedented took place on Saturday
afternoon in the composing-room of the Daily Post
office, the object of the meeting being to present to Mr M
J Whitty, the venerated founder of this journal, a
testimonial of the admiration and affection with which he
is regarded. It was natural that Mr Whitty's withdrawal
from the conduct and proprietorship of the Daily Post
should suggest the desirableness of some such
demonstration, and Mr Whitty was with some reluctance
prevailed upon to accept the honour when it was
proposed that a testimonial should be presented to him

by those who had been engaged under his direction in the various departments of the office. The compositors were most active in furthering the scheme, but it was united in by the employees of every department, and representative names were attached to the testimonial, which took the form of an address, most exquisitely engrossed and illuminated by Mr Dyall, of the Lyceum, whose success in this species of art has several times been conspicuously exhibited on similar occasions of public interest. Mr Whitty attended at half-past five o'clock to receive the address, accompanied by Miss Whitty, Miss Mary Whitty, and Master Michael Whitty, and was received with an overwhelming demonstration by an assemblage of the employees, in all numbering about a hundred persons.

The Nation, 12 October 1872 (R60). Whitty published in 1824, two volumes of *Tales of Irish Life*, which included a thinly veiled account of the alleged murder of Ellen Hanley in 1819 at the hands of John Scanlan and Stephen Sullivan, entitled 'The Poor Man's Daughter'. Reproduced in 2012 by Janet Murphy and Eileen Chamberlain as *The Poor Man's Daughter: A Return to the Colleen Bawn*, it is available at www.lulu.com

AN IRISH writer who is utterly forgotten but who achieved some fame in his time was Michael James Whitty, a native of Wexford, where his father owned some trading vessels. Whitty went to London in his early twenties and embarked upon a literary career. His first book was an anonymous production entitled "Tales of Irish Life" for which the illustrations were supplied by the celebrated George Cruikshank. It had a big success, and was translated into French and German, as well as being reprinted in America. After editing various periodicals, Whitty removed to Liverpool, where, before he was forty, he became Chief Constable of the city. He organised the first provincial police force and gave Liverpool its first fire brigade. In 1855 he founded the *Liverpool Daily Post*, the first penny paper to appear in Britain for 200 years. Many of his scattered writings were collected and published in volume form in 1870, including some papers on Robert Emmet. These latter, however, were the fruit of imagination rather than knowledge. Whitty died on June 10 1873 in his seventy-eighth year.

Barry Sullivan's Generosity: The death of Charles Cavanagh, Theatre Royal boxkeeper, a worthy and obliging official, reminds me of a matter in which he had some part. In days long past Barry Sullivan had received kindness and consideration from Michael James Whitty, a Liverpool newspaper proprietor of large influence. A relative of Mr Whitty, of the same name, and who was an able journalist, died in Melbourne, and his remains lay in a nameless grave. When the actor [Barry Sullivan] became cognisant of this he expended £100 in erecting a monument over that grave, and year by year he has transmitted to Mr Cavanagh, in whose charge he left it, a sum for its proper maintenance. It was Mr Sullivan I think who with keen managerial instinct, first gave Mr Cavanagh a responsible appointment, a choice amply justified since. (*The Nation*, 2 August 1879)

WINDELE, John (1801-1865)

JOHN WINDELE was one of the very small remnant of a once numerous band of citizens who by their own cultivation and taste, influenced to a considerable extent the intellectual character of our city. Engaged in the dullest routine of official life – that of the sheriff's office – the mind of John Windele was not allowed to stagnate in the monotony of his daily drudgery. An eager thirster after knowledge, he directed much of the energy of his mind to antiquarian pursuits. He explored ancient abbeys, and towers, and raths, and deciphered almost extinct letters and carvings upon shattered crosses and time-worn monuments of a ruder type. We doubt if there was a man in the country who was more thoroughly acquainted with its topography or who had a wider knowledge of its mouldering ruins than John Windele. He was a recognised authority on all matters appertaining to the history, annals, and traditions of his native land, and his verdict upon any moot question was held in respect by such men as Petrie, Curry or O'Donovan. He was an honoured member of the Archaeological Society of Kilkenny, to which he contributed several valuable papers. He wrote with facility and with remarkable purity. At times his humour was delightfully genial, and his quizzing sketches of his own friends were hit off with exquisite drollery, in which the warmth of the heart was as evident as the gleam of the spirit. His 'History of Cork' is a valuable addition to our local literature; and his 'Guide to Killarney' has been and yet will be most useful to those who live upon the brains of their fellows. And what a collector our departed friend was! There is no eminent man of whom he had not some valuable record in his scrap books, rather his scrap books. Years and the loss of dear friends and cherished companions worked their effect on John Windele, imparting to his manner and tone of thought a gravity not natural to him, for we can remember the time when he was the life and soul of the country ramble and the social entertainment, and the promoter of pleasant fun and harmless joke; that is, when Father Mat Horgan, of Blarney and Abraham Able, and William Kelleher, were alive. But these days are gone, and the last of that genial band has followed those whom he loved, and by whom he was beloved. Had not the disease smote brain and body, it is quite possible that John Windele would have added much to his reputation by some works of greater pretension than those which he produced, for the love of writing was strong in him, as it is with most men of his class who love literature for its own sake. But alas! The fatal bolt has been sped, and his labours are over in this world. There are few, indeed, who knew him that will not think kindly of his memory, as not only was he a man of gentle manners and blameless life, but he was one of those who assisted, and in no mean degree either, to uphold the literary taste and intellectual repute of his native city.

Edited from *Freeman's Journal*, 1 September 1865 (R31)

WILSON, Ellen Josephine (1898-1975) nee Lilburn, daughter of William Lilburn and Catherine Moriarty whose grandfather Jeremiah Moriarty was native of Ballybunion, died at her home in Deptford, London at the age of 77 on 31 March 1975 from heart failure and was buried at Grove Park Cemetery, London on April 14 1975 following a private service attended by family members

ELLEN JOSEPHINE, my grandmother, was aged 12 years and one of seven children when her mother died young. Ellen was put in a workhouse in London and this is as much as I know of her childhood and upbringing. Her brother Henry Lilburn was killed in Belgium in 1917 during the First World War at the Battle of Passchendaele. Ellen married Frederick Ernest Wilson and had three children. My father, Ronald, the youngest, arrived some 12 years after his sister Constance and brother Len. Ellen died when I was about 12 years old and my memories of her are visits to our home on a Saturday afternoon, arriving by bus in a large overcoat with curious looking fox-fur collar and hat, sitting on the sofa with her skirt hitched up showing her long-johns. She always brought sweets from Deptford market for me and my two brothers and sister and on an occasional Sunday we would visit her in her high-rise London flat with my dad, we would have to dress up and as children we loved going up in the lift if it was working or mounting the graffiti lined concrete staircase. We would sit quietly and mannerly in her highly polished living room, afraid to move, listening to the tick of the clock while she chatted with my dad. She once gave me a small glass of port, and laughed with my dad as I sipped it and shuddered! When their backs were turned I emptied it in the plant pot and then worried the plant would die and I would be found out. Sometimes I sat with her in her tiny kitchen and played with her bag of hair-rollers at her table while she cooked and told me stories of her exploits with her sister Kitty when she was a girl. She told me to always remember she would look over me from heaven when she died, that she would be my guardian angel. From her jewellery box she gave me an old photo mounted in a badge of my dad in uniform and two coins, a penny dated 1902 and a halfpenny dated 1929 which she wrapped in a piece of paper on which she had written 'for Janet from nan'. I was seven years old then. She told me to treasure those items; I still have the badge, the coins have disappeared, but the scrap of paper in her hand is the most valued of all.

Obituary composed 1st September 2010 by Janet Murphy, grand-daughter of deceased (R1). See memoir, *The Chronicles of a Lorry Driver being those of Ronald Dennis Wilson* at www.lulu.com

WISE, Captain

CAPTAIN WISE, whose death has occasioned a great
gloom in Killarney, and indeed prevented the gentry
from giving a stag hunt in honour of the great Northern
Bard [Sir Walter Scott], was a brother of the gentleman
who married a daughter of Lucien Buonaparte. Capt
Wise met his death under somewhat extraordinary
circumstances. There is a sporting club in Killarney,
consisting of the gentlemen in the neighbourhood. The
members of this club met a few days ago to determine
upon the toasts that should be given for the ensuing
season. The health of the Duke of York was objected to,
on the ground of his having opposed the Catholic
Claims. One gentleman, however, was desirous that the
Duke's health should be drank as a private gentleman.
This was warmly opposed by Capt Wise, who concluded
his objection by observing, 'that his Royal Highness had

trampled upon their religion.' The word 'religion' was scarcely out of the unfortunate gentleman's mouth when he fell upon the ground, and almost instantaneously expired.

Morning Post, 16 August 1829 (R59) NB: Perhaps related to Sir Thomas Wyse, KCB, MP, of Waterford, Ireland (pictured above), British Minister to Athens, prominent Catholic leader and author of *History of the Catholic Association,* who was married to Letitia, daughter of Lucien Bonaparte.

YUDENITCH, Flora (Sandes)

MISS FLORA Sandes, who died recently at the age of 80, served for seven years from 1915 in the Serbian Army as a fighting soldier and was decorated for her bravery in the field. She was the youngest daughter of the Rev Samuel Dickson Sandes, rector of Whitechurch, Co Cork who later moved to England, where she was born. She was adventurous by nature and learnt to ride and shoot and, in the days when motoring was an adventure and not just a means of transport, acquired an old French racing car. In such ways she relieved the monotony during the period when she had to earn her living as a secretary in a London office. At the beginning of the 1914-18 War, having been a member of the St John Ambulance Brigade for some years, she had a chance to go out to Serbia with a small nursing unit. She later joined the Serbian Red Cross, and when the Bulgarians invaded Serbia, she obtained permission to join the ambulance of the 2nd Infantry Regiment as a dresser. The Serbian Army was slowly being driven back by overwhelming odds with their only line of retreat through the Albanian Mountains, and conditions were such that Miss Sandes drifted by successive stages from a nurse into a soldier. The soldiers with the ambulance took it for granted that anyone who could ride and shoot would be a soldier under such conditions, and it was not unusual for Serbian peasant girls to fight with the army. When, therefore, they reached country impassable to ambulances she took the Red Cross badge off her arm and said she would join the 2nd Regiment as a private. The procedure was simple; the colonel took the little brass regimental figures off his own epaulettes and fastened them on the shoulder straps of his new recruit, and official sanction came a little later. She was regarded as a considerable asset, for the simple peasant soldiers looked on her as a representative of England and a pledge that in the end England would help them. But their personal affection for her soon increased almost to idolatry, for under the stress of war she showed all the qualities they most admired – outstanding courage, cheerfulness, and sympathy. Her service with the Serbian Army lasted seven years and she experienced the hardest conditions of mountain warfare, with terrible losses, through defeat and victory until the general demobilization in the autumn of 1922. The 2nd Regiment was known as the 'Iron Regiment' and spent most of its time in the front lien where she fought in every battle until she was severely wounded by a Bulgarian hand grenade in November 1916. Sergeant Sandes, as she then was, was taken to a British military field hospital for Serbians, where she remained for about two months, and where she was decorated by the aide-de-camp of the Prince Regent with the Order of the Kara-George – a rare decoration given for conspicuous bravery in the field. She was given sick leave in England, where she raised more funds and collected comforts for the Serbian soldiers, and in May 1917, she returned to her regiment and took part in all further operations. She was given a commission in June 1919, and promoted to lieutenant on demobilization in 1922, and in 1926 she received the rank of captain. In 1927 she married Yurie Yudenitch, who had been a colonel in the White Russian Army and had escaped from Russia during the revolution. He joined the Serbian army as a sergeant and had been in her regiment. They lived in France for a time and later in Belgrade where during the last war they were both interned by the Germans. They were later released on parole. They had little to live on, but she had her army pension and taught English. Her husband died in 1941 and at the end of the German occupation, she settled in England in a small cottage in Suffolk where she lived until her death.

The Times, 1 December 1956 (R50)

INDEX OF OBITUARIES